YORK NOTES

Saint Joan

George Bernard Shaw

Note by Dr Julian Cowley

Longman   York Press

Dr Julian Cowley is hereby identified as author of this work in accordance with
Section 77 of the Copyright, Designs and Patents Act 1988

YORK PRESS
322 Old Brompton Road, London SW5 9JH

PEARSON EDUCATION LIMITED
Edinburgh Gate, Harlow,
Essex CM20 2JE, United Kingdom
Associated companies, branches and representatives throughout the world

First published 2000

ISBN 0–582–42456–9

Designed by Vicki Pacey
Phototypeset by Gem Graphics, Trenance, Mawgan Porth, Cornwall
Colour reproduction and film output by Spectrum Colour
Produced by Addison Wesley Longman China Limited, Hong Kong

CONTENTS

PART ONE

INTRODUCTION

HOW TO STUDY A PLAY

Studying on your own requires self-discipline and a carefully thought-out work plan in order to be effective.

- Drama is a special kind of writing (the technical term is 'genre') because it needs a performance in the theatre to arrive at a full interpretation of its meaning. Try to imagine that you are a member of the audience when reading the play. Think about how it could be presented on the stage, not just about the words on the page.

- Drama is often about conflict of some sort (which may be below the surface). Identify the conflicts in the play and you will be close to identifying the large ideas or themes which bind all the parts together.

- Make careful notes on themes, character, plot and any subplots of the play.

- Why do you like or dislike the characters in the play? How do your feelings towards them develop and change?

- Playwrights find non-realistic ways of allowing an audience to see into the minds and motives of their characters, for example **soliloquy**, aside or music. Consider how such dramatic devices are used in the play.

- Think of the playwright writing the play. Why were these particular arrangements of events, characters and speeches chosen?

- Cite exact sources for all quotations, whether from the text itself or from critical commentaries. Wherever possible find your own examples from the play to back up your own opinions.

- Always express your ideas in your own words.

This York Note offers an introduction to *Saint Joan* and cannot substitute for close reading of the text and the study of secondary sources.

In 1920, Joan of Arc was made a saint by the Roman Catholic Church. Three years later, George Bernard Shaw's play *Saint Joan* received its first performance, to critical acclaim. It confirmed George Bernard Shaw's status as one of the most accomplished living dramatists, and has come to be widely regarded as the peak of his long career. Not the least important aspect of the play is that it has provided one of the few notable major roles in twentieth-century drama for performance by a young actress. It continues to be produced regularly.

Reading *Saint Joan*, it is important to bear in mind that it was written specifically for the stage, but taken apart from that context it still has plenty to offer us, in its lively characterisation and dialogue, and in its engagement with serious ideas concerning values that have prevailed in Western European societies since the Middle Ages.

For George Bernard Shaw, Joan represented the emergence of a particularly modern conception of individuality. **Ironically,** given her recent canonisation by the Vatican, this conception was closely linked to the rise of Protestant Christianity, and George Bernard Shaw's Joan is a characterful precursor of Protestant belief. She can also be seen as the herald of nationalism, foreshadowing the arrival of a dramatically new political organisation throughout Europe.

This is a great deal to place upon the shoulders of an illiterate teenager from the French countryside, and any critical reading needs to evaluate the extent of George Bernard Shaw's success in creating a credible character, who yet carries such weighty historical significance. In the published text, our approach to the play is prepared by a characteristically strident Preface, which puts forward George Bernard Shaw's main arguments in the play, and addresses some points of adverse criticism which followed early performances. Here the dramatist outlines his philosophical belief in a Life Force, and suggests how Joan's case might cast light on such diverse issues as the political militancy of early twentieth-century feminists, and the crisis in Ireland at the time of the First World War.

George Bernard Shaw was an intellectual playwright, but he has also been an extremely popular one. This is a rare combination, requiring an unusual set of skills. *Saint Joan*, arguably more than any other of his plays, is a rich resource for studying one of the finest practitioners of modern drama at work.

PART TWO

SUMMARIES & COMMENTARIES

George Bernard Shaw began writing *Saint Joan* on 29 April 1923, and had finished it by the end of August. It is subtitled, 'A Chronicle Play in Six Scenes and an Epilogue'. The first English edition was published by Constable, in London, in 1924. In the same year, a German translation appeared in Berlin.

Between 1930 and 1932 Constable issued a *Collected Edition* of George Bernard Shaw's works, which of course included *Saint Joan*. The play was also part of the *Standard Edition*, which Constable published between 1937 and 1949. *Saint Joan* was first issued as a Penguin paperback in 1946. The current Penguin edition, used for this Note, offers the definitive text, edited by Dan H. Laurence, and appears as part of 'The Bernard Shaw Library'. The omission of apostrophes from contractions such as 'isn't' and 'don't' is in accordance with George Bernard Shaw's instruction. George Bernard Shaw wrote the Preface, which occupies forty pages of this edition, in May 1924.

The play was first performed by the Theatre Guild, at the Garrick Theatre, New York, on 28 December 1923. The British première took place at the New Theatre, London, on 26 March 1924, with Sybil Thorndike cast as Joan.

George Bernard Shaw wanted a film version to be made, and in 1934 he wrote a screen adaptation of *Saint Joan*. The project ran into financial difficulties, and met with some opposition from Catholic groups, and it was abandoned. The screenplay can be read in *The Collected Screenplays of Bernard Shaw* (George Prior, 1980). A film of the play was eventually made in 1957, directed by Otto Preminger, with a screenplay by the Catholic novelist, Graham Greene.

SYNOPSIS

In 1429, a young country girl named Joan arrives at the castle of Squire Robert de Baudricourt, seeking his practical assistance for her mission to crown the Dauphin as King of France. Initially he is dismissive but, hearing more of the widespread belief that she is a worker of miracles, he is soon won over. Despite his reluctance to grant authority to the saintly voices bearing messages from God, which she claims to hear, he is persuaded to support her efforts to raise the siege at Orleans, and to secure the coronation of Charles VII.

Joan proceeds to Chinon, where the Dauphin holds court. He is a timid character, largely held in disdain by the powerful nobility. Joan uses her powers of persuasion to overcome the hostility and scepticism of the nobles and the clergy, and to convince the diffident Charles that he might yet be king. He grants her command of his forces.

Near Orleans, she meets Jack Dunois, leader of the French forces, and announces her intention to lift the siege of that city, and to drive the English troops out of France. Dunois points out the tactical problem posed by adverse wind direction. Suddenly, the wind switches, enabling an effective attack to be staged. Dunois senses divine intervention and pledges allegiance to Joan.

Following the liberation of Orleans, the Earl of Warwick and the chaplain to his troops meet with Peter Cauchon, the Bishop of Beauvais, in the English camp, to discuss the threat posed by Joan. There have been other defeats, following the lifting of the siege. Warwick and the bishop hatch a plan whereby, after her capture by the English, Joan will be handed over to the Church for trial as a heretic.

Charles is crowned in Rheims Cathedral, and Joan declares her mission accomplished. Amid a general sentiment of relief that she plans to return home, Joan changes her mind, and expresses her intention to capture Paris, and her resolution to expel the English invaders from her native land.

By May 1431, Joan has been captured, and submitted for trial by an ecclesiastical court. The court assembles in a castle in Rouen. A member of the Inquisition insists that the main charge to be pursued is that of heresy. Joan is adamant that her personal communication with God's saints takes precedence over the orthodox beliefs of the Church. Bishop Cauchon is appalled by this heretical position. Eventually, the likelihood of execution is raised, and Joan agrees to sign a recantation of her former beliefs. She withdraws this when she realises that the alternative to execution is lifelong imprisonment.

Joan is excommunicated, then led to the stake to be burnt. The executioner reports to Warwick that her incinerated remains have been cast into the river. Her heart, however, would not burn.

The Epilogue occurs twenty-five years later. The case has been reconsidered, and the original verdict has been overturned. Martin Ladvenu, a monk, visits the king's bedchamber to report this reversal, which pleases Charles as it restores authority to his reign. Joan's spirit then appears in the room, followed by the ghost of Cauchon, complaining about the vilification to which he has been retrospectively subjected.

The image of Dunois then appears, although the soldier is actually asleep in his bed at Chateaudun. A soldier, who made a makeshift cross for Joan during the burning, visits the chamber, temporarily released from hell. Chaplain de Stogumber appears and testifies to the horror of the execution, which continues to haunt him even though he now lives as a priest in a quiet parish. Finally, a representative of the modern Church appears and announces the canonisation of Joan by the Vatican. All these figures pay homage to the young woman, but when she aspires to return to life they all cower and slink away, horrified at the prospect of another incarnation for this agent of disruption and change. At the end of the play, Joan is alone, pondering the future of humanity.

Preface

Saint Joan is a drama that addresses ideas, and George Bernard Shaw supplied a lengthy Preface in order to clarify and extend the play's philosophical concerns. Written in May 1924, following the play's first London performance in March, these notes enabled the playwright to respond to his critics in a manner which ensured that his views would permanently accompany the text of *Saint Joan*.

George Bernard Shaw pointedly refers to the Preface as 'a sober essay on the facts' (p. 39). While he deals at length with historical issues and their implications, he says very little about the staging of the play. Perhaps he felt that, at this point in his career, his approach to dramatic writing required no further commentary. Still, the effect of the Preface is to shift attention away from the accomplishment of George Bernard Shaw's stagecraft, towards his intellectual concerns. It is important to remember that *Saint Joan* was written to be performed; any reading of the play should take that into account.

The following notes retain the headings that George Bernard Shaw used to subdivide his prefatory essay:

Joan the Original and Presumptuous

Joan of Arc was born about 1412, and was burnt as a heretic and a witch in 1431. George Bernard Shaw considers her subsequent reputation. He argues that she was a precursor of modern practices in dress and in warfare, and, significantly, he identifies her as the first Protestant and the first nationalist.

He notes that she was burnt to death while still in her teens, for offences no longer recognised as such in our changed society. But he suggests that her true crime was essentially 'unwomanly and insufferable presumption' (p. 7). Her self-confidence, or arrogance, according to one's point of view, meant that she respected no source of authority other than her own understanding of God's intentions. Her youthfulness made her seem still more of an upstart. George Bernard Shaw observes that there were two basic views of her: 'One was that she was miraculous: the other that she was unbearable' (p. 7).

George Bernard Shaw, after giving key dates in Joan's history, culminating in her canonisation as a saint only four years earlier, refers to her as 'the queerest fish among the eccentric worthies of the Middle Ages' (p. 7). Colloquial irreverence is continued into her characterisation: Joan speaks with similarly lively informality. The playwright regards her as a profoundly serious figure, nonetheless, and much of what follows in the Preface is designed to establish her relevance for readers and audiences in the twentieth century.

George Bernard Shaw presents Joan as a vital agent of change. His view of the world had come to centre on belief in a Life Force. This was an impersonal drive which shaped history, but which required receptive human beings in order to do its work for the eventual improvement of life on earth (see Theme on Creative Evolution and the Life Force). Joan is an appropriately receptive figure, an agent of evolution, initiating two strands of advanced thinking: Protestantism and nationalism.

Joan considered herself a pious Roman Catholic, but George Bernard Shaw argues that her rejection of the institutional authority of the Church, and her refusal to allow priests to mediate between her and divine revelation, formed the core of what later became known as Protestantism. In Protestant Christianity the individual assumed far greater importance than in medieval Roman Catholicism. As he goes on to remark, 'the supremacy of private judgment for the individual' is 'the quintessence of Protestantism' (p. 29). George Bernard Shaw is suggesting that Joan was a pivotal figure in the development of reverence for the individual, a crucial aspect of Western Europe's adoption of modern values.

Her nationalism was similarly a shift away from the long-established feudal order, in which powerful lords held sway over the local peasantry. In that system there was no room for the notions of individual liberty that form the cornerstone of modern democratic societies. Boundaries between countries were far less significant than the ties that bound Europe's ruling classes together. Power was eventually transferred away from feudal lords, and was invested in a monarch who exercised central control. This led to the formation of modern national identities, and relationships between social classes became far more flexible. Gradually, the peasantry became citizens with rights as well as obligations.

George Bernard Shaw's Joan sees the crowning of Charles as an affirmation of national pride, which cuts across class divisions. The French lords in the play feel affinity with their English counterparts, but Joan disregards such class allegiance and presents the conflict as a matter of France versus England. This is a modern conception of nationhood which, as George Bernard Shaw recognises, would have been alien to Joan's contemporaries.

Linking Joan with Napoleon, George Bernard Shaw highlights the infrequency with which such exceptional agents of evolutionary change appear within human society. Joan is seen as a precursor of the French emperor in her 'realism' in warfare. Medieval combat had far fewer serious political implications.

The way in which George Bernard Shaw writes of Joan's self-confident dismissal of all recognised authority suggests his own close identification with her. He readily assumed the role of sage and prophet, and was not content to be regarded merely as a writer of diverting plays.

the Vosges mountainous area of Lorraine, in France

Husites followers of Jan Hus, sometimes spelled Huss (*c.*1369–1415) a religious reformer from Bohemia, now part of the Czech Republic. He taught at the University of Prague, but was later burnt as a heretic

rational dressing for women a Rational Dress Society, formed in England in 1881, promoted the wearing of clothing that did not restrict movement or impair health. It was especially opposed to tight corsets and heavy skirts

Queen Christina of Sweden (1626–89), ruled Sweden from 1644 until 1654. She was renowned for her learning and knowledge of the arts. She abdicated following her conversion to Roman Catholicism, a faith then proscribed in Sweden

Catalina de Erauso seventeenth-century Basque woman, who dressed as a man and lived the life of a solider and adventurer

the Church Triumphant Christians in heaven

Cassius Gaius Cassius Longinus (d.42BC) played a major role in the assassination of Julius Caesar in 44BC

Joan and Socrates

Joan's youthful innocence makes her an attractive historical figure, although she might have lived longer had she possessed more guile. George Bernard Shaw cites the Greek philosopher Socrates as a wise man whose persecution was a measure of widespread ignorance. He notes how 'mental superiority' is despised, even when it produces beneficial advice, offered with good will (p. 8).

It is crucial to George Bernard Shaw's characterisation that Joan's directness and honesty are seen to be positive qualities, despite being met with disapproval. Her unsophisticated frankness is a virtue, but in another light it can be seen as unworldly tactlessness, which precipitated her early death.

The philosopher Socrates is associated with wisdom acquired through age and experience. Despite the contrast in their ages, he and Joan are linked through their fate. Both died as a result of persecution by those in authority. Both were also, in George Bernard Shaw's view, important agents of evolutionary change (see Theme on Creative Evolution and the Life Force).

Here, George Bernard Shaw makes the reference to ancient Greece relevant to his contemporaries through allusion to suburban railways, a familiar phenomenon in 1924. He is making the case of Socrates germane to the present, while hinting that democratic citizens of the twentieth century remain in need of guidance from a sage, although they may feel hostile to that idea. Exceptional figures are invariably despised, even when their intentions are entirely beneficent. It is likely that George Bernard Shaw is drawing this conclusion from his own experiences, fuelled by his sense of his own historical importance. He had fallen from favour during the previous decade on account of writings in which he had criticised the government's conduct of the First World War. He still felt bitter at the opprobrium to which he had been subjected.

Queen Elizabeth Elizabeth I (1533–1603) ruled England from 1558 until her death

Socrates (469–399BC), an immensely influential Athenian philosopher, who made character and conduct his objects of study. He was sentenced to death for neglect of the gods and for unconventional religious practices. He chose to take his own life by drinking hemlock

Contrast with Napoleon

After further comparison of Joan with Socrates, George Bernard Shaw refers again to Napoleon who, lacking their essential innocence, was aware of the trepidation he caused. George Bernard Shaw notes that 'Fear will drive men to any extreme', and he observes that conventional figures of authority, however powerful, are less likely to inspire fear than those 'mental giants' whose power defies easy rationalisation. He concludes that 'it is far more dangerous to be a saint than to be a conqueror' (p. 9). He mentions Mahomet and Joan as combining these roles, and remarks how Joan had no supporters to rally to her defence at the time of her execution.

> George Bernard Shaw has linked Joan with Napoleon, as a later French military leader who saw himself as a shaper of the world's destiny. The two are differentiated in that Napoleon's political ambitions are more readily comprehensible than the visionary intensity that motivated Joan. George Bernard Shaw is suggesting that while power may reside in an emperor, greater power inheres in the actions of figures such as Saint Joan and the great prophet of Islam, whose aspirations are not constrained by the material conditions of the world. Isolation and incomprehension may be the immediate price to be paid for a more enduring influence on the course of human history.

Herod and Pilate Herod was a ruler in the province of Galilee at the time of Christ's birth; Pontius Pilate was the governor of Judea who sentenced Christ to death

Annas and Caiaphas Jewish high priests in Jerusalem at the time of Christ

Was Joan Innocent or Guilty?

Joan was found unequivocally guilty by her contemporaries. She was rehabilitated in 1456, in order to ensure the legitimacy of the coronation of Charles VII, formerly the Dauphin. More recently, historians have come to regard those who conducted the original trial as criminal in their treatment of her. George Bernard Shaw contests this view of their guilt. Still, the evidence presented in the 1456 proceedings testified to Joan's pious and moderate character, and demonstrated the inappropriateness of viewing her as a witch. She was quite distinct from the heroines to be found in popular **melodramas**. Her crucial failings, George Bernard Shaw suggests, were pride and presumption.

> George Bernard Shaw is keen to preserve Joan's character from idealisation, which would place her outside the sphere of normal human experience. Equally, he is eager to rescue her judges from latter-day accusations of blind prejudice. His portrayal of Peter Cauchon has generated considerable critical discussion, and research has indicated that George Bernard Shaw actually

suppressed his own awareness of the bishop's corruption. Why should the dramatist wish to show Joan's persecutors in a more moderate light? The principal reason is probably that George Bernard Shaw wanted to avoid perception of the trial as a simple conflict of good and evil. Rather, he required a basically benevolent old regime to be superseded by a vibrant new order, driven by the Life Force, with Joan the necessary agent. The trial is to be seen as a key historical turning point, not just a matter of timeless moral conflict.

As indicated here, George Bernard Shaw felt that Protestants had come to use the burning of Joan as a blunt instrument with which to bludgeon the Roman Catholic Church and the Inquisition: 'The easiest way to make these institutions the villains of a melodrama was to make The Maid its heroine. That melodrama may be dismissed as rubbish' (p. 10). In avoiding **melodrama** he goes so far as to assert that Joan's trial was more fair than that an accused person of her kind receives in a modern secular court. It is likely that he had in mind the trial of Roger Casement and of the leaders of the Irish Nationalist cause, whom George Bernard Shaw had supported, and who had recently been executed by the British government (see Historical Background – Irish Nationalism).

George Bernard Shaw seeks to rescue the terms 'genius' and 'saint' from unworldly associations. A 'genius' is a far-sighted and profound individual who makes 'ethical evaluations' beyond those of which most people are capable. Energy to put insight into practical effect is crucially a factor in the formation of a genius. A saint is someone who has 'practised heroic virtues' and has experienced 'revelations or powers', whom the Catholic Church deems worthy of canonisation. George Bernard Shaw does not allow that these revelations and powers are of themselves supernatural in the sense that the Church endorses. Nonetheless, he argues that strict rationalism, which places its faith squarely in the processes of conscious reasoning, is inadequate to comprehend the inspirational understanding manifested in the saint's actions. George Bernard Shaw is here implicitly defending his belief in a Life Force at work in the world through the agency of receptive human beings (see Theme on Creative Evolution and the Life Force). The emphasis is on active engagement with the world.

George Bernard Shaw introduces gender politics with his reference to an 'Anti-Feminist' historian excluding women from any account of human achievement. Nineteenth-century orthodoxies in writing history, with their bias against women, needed to be replaced with a twentieth-century mode of historiography

capable of throwing off sex partialities and their romance, and regarding woman as the female of the human species, and not as a different kind of animal with specific charms and specific imbecilities. (p. 11)

Part of George Bernard Shaw's agenda in *Saint Joan* was to deploy historical data in ways that did not perpetuate a bias against the social and cultural significance of women (see Theme on Women's Rights, and Historical Background – Contemporary Feminism).

Jingo patriotism aggressively chauvinistic nationalism, after a popular song of the 1870s which proclaimed, 'We don't want to fight, but by Jingo if we do ...'

Joan's Good Looks

Her contemporaries remarked upon Joan's plainness; that historical testimony distinguishes her clearly from stereotypical heroines of literary **romance·**

George Bernard Shaw's Joan is not a figure out of popular **melodrama;** nor is she the characteristically beautiful heroine of romance. Some critics, including Raymond Williams, have accused George Bernard Shaw of rendering Joan sexless. But long before such objections were raised, the playwright, in his Preface, furnished a response: Joan was not sexless, and did not exclude the possibility of marriage. In fact, her early death precluded it, while during her lifetime she was preoccupied with a more significant mission than the search for a husband. George Bernard Shaw was conscious of the absence of overt sexuality, which Williams later noted, but preferred to keep his historical account free from such distractions.

George Bernard Shaw refers to picture postcards to help contemporary readers perceive Joan's relevance to modern issues. She would have been represented on them as a general. This emphasises the important challenge she posed to gender stereotypes. No woman had had access to such a rank during the recent First World War.

The playwright supports the view that a statue made in Orleans, of a young woman wearing a helmet, depicts Joan. He remarks that it was a singular work of art for its day, in that it was evidently a realistic portrait rather than an idealised image. This clearly has relevance to his own attempts, centuries later, to purge the popular sense of Joan of Arc of any vestiges of romantic idealisation. Such efforts are characteristic of his overall approach to writing drama.

Byron's formula a quotation from *Don Juan* (1819–21), Canto I, Stanza 194, written by the poet Lord Byron (1788–1824)

Joan's Social Position

Joan was a farmer's daughter, raised in a feudal society. She belonged to the middle ranks, and resented being identified as a shepherdess. George Bernard Shaw compares the social context of her upbringing with that of William Shakespeare. In summary, he concludes that Joan was 'much more of a young lady, and even of an intellectual, than most of the daughters of our petty bourgeoisie' (p. 13).

After attending to gender issues raised by Joan's story, George Bernard Shaw now turns to matters of social class. He locates Joan firmly in the middle ranks, in touch with the peasantry, yet at ease in the company of the ruling class. Again, this suits his realistic purpose, because the 'facts leave us no excuse for the popular romance that turns every heroine into either a princess or a beggar-maid' (p. 12). Writers of **romantic** fantasies are attracted to extremes; George Bernard Shaw wishes to convey the dramatic and political potential latent within the routines of normal daily life.

Earlier, George Bernard Shaw compared Joan to Socrates, Mahomet and Napoleon. Now he associates her with William Shakespeare, another signal historical figure. A romanticised version of Shakespeare's life has him miraculously transformed from illiterate to genius. George Bernard Shaw affirms that his eminent predecessor was in fact the son of a businessman. He came, therefore, from the middle ranks, like Joan. George Bernard Shaw is insistent that the middle classes, to which he himself belonged, have the capacity to effect radical social change. If members of that group prove receptive to the Life Force, they will play a key role in social evolution. This view contrasts with the Marxist model underpinning the revolution that had recently occurred in Russia. There the peasant class was entrusted with historical change. George Bernard Shaw did admire the revolutionary leader Lenin, however, as he was later to admire figures on the political right, as agents of historical development (see Historical Background – The Russian Revolution).

Shakespeare was a literate man, and thus well suited to make an impact through literature. Joan, on the other hand, was entirely illiterate, and had to adopt other means to make her historical mark. She became a soldier and a political leader, while remaining a visionary. In fact, she did overcome her inability to read or write by dictating letters, but George Bernard Shaw stresses that illiteracy should not be equated with ignorance. It was a deficiency in accord with the prevailing condition of European society in her day. Reading and writing was almost exclusively the province of churchmen.

George Bernard Shaw compares Joan favourably, in her understanding of contemporary politics, to 'most of our newspaper fed university women-graduates' (p. 12). But in order, once again, to preclude the assumption that she was supernaturally gifted, he explains: 'This knowledge of and interest in public affairs was nothing extraordinary among farmers in a war-swept countryside' (p. 12). This necessary alertness to pressing political realities, with tangible day-to-day consequences, is contrasted with the dulling effect, as George Bernard Shaw saw it, of reading the daily press in twentieth-century Britain.

Shakespear   George Bernard Shaw consistently adopts this variant spelling of Shakespeare's name

Joan's Voices and Visions

Joan's reputation has been inseparable from reference to the mystical visions and voices she experienced. These have been taken as proof of her madness, inauthenticity, sorcery, and finally her saintliness. George Bernard Shaw refers to scientist Isaac Newton's mystical tendencies, and insists that this aspect of Joan's experience should not discredit or compromise her important contribution to the history of European civilisation.

> George Bernard Shaw takes widely varying interpretations of Joan's visionary experience as evidence that narrowly rational historians have arrived at only a limited understanding of her. He attributes her mysticism to a highly active imagination, and observes that this can lead to criminal activity, but also to 'The inspirations and intuitions and unconsciously reasoned conclusions of genius' (p. 13). He is eager to salvage these inspired discoveries from accusations of insanity, and forcibly argues that 'The test of sanity is not the normality of the method but the reasonableness of the discovery' (p. 13). This variation upon the view that ends justify means also informed some of George Bernard Shaw's less palatable political positions. At times, he advocated purging society of undesirable elements in the manner practised by totalitarian governments.

> Physicist Isaac Newton is added to the pantheon of recognised great figures that George Bernard Shaw is assembling for comparison with Joan. Isaac Newton's fame is assured by his contribution to scientific knowledge, but he was a man equally inclined to mysticism and arcane investigations. By analogy, the more picturesque aspects of Joan's story should not be allowed to diminish her enduring contribution as the first Protestant and the first nationalist.

> George Bernard Shaw cites recent experiences of women serving during the First World War in support of the necessity for Joan to wear conventionally masculine clothing. It was a matter of common sense, irrespective of her claim that she was ordered by a saint's voice to dress in this way. Her strategy in restoring the Dauphin to

the throne was similarly in accordance with common sense, even though it was sanctioned by an auditory hallucination; such plans might have been conceived 'by Napoleon or any other illusionproof genius' (p. 14).

Luther Martin Luther (1483–1546), a German religious reformer, historically the founder of Protestantism, and so a major figure in the history of Christianity

Swedenborg Emanuel Swedenborg (1688–1772), a Swedish scientist, engineer, philosopher and mystic

Blake William Blake (1757–1827), an English poet, painter and visionary

Saint Francis (c.1181–1226), the visionary son of a merchant, born in Assisi, Italy. In 1210 he founded the Franciscan friars, an order devoted to poverty and charitable service. He was canonised in 1228

Newton Sir Isaac Newton (1642–1727), epochal physicist who, as George Bernard Shaw points out, manifested an obsessive interest in the more arcane areas of Christian belief, and wrote commentaries on the Book of Revelation and other prophetic books, including that attributed to Daniel

Pythagoras (c.582–c.507BC), Greek mathematician, who championed a philosophy which upheld belief in the transmigration of souls

the Copernican version the model of the solar system as centred on the Sun, with the Earth and other planets moving around it, formulated by Nicolaus Copernicus (1473–1543)

a Bedlamite king Bedlam was the popular name for the hospital of St Mary of Bethlehem, the first English asylum for the insane, initially founded in London in 1247

Saint Catherine Catherine of Alexandria, said to have died early in the fourth century AD, was an educated young noblewoman who protested against persecutions under the Roman Empire. As a consequence, she was tortured on a spiked wheel before being beheaded

The Evolutionary Appetite

George Bernard Shaw declares that as he was born into the Victorian age and into a Protestant family he cannot personally accept the objective existence of the three saints who counselled Joan. His view is that they were, in fact, projections of her receptiveness to the Life Force, which he identifies as an 'evolutionary appetite' (p. 15).

The essential point being made here is that each age interprets events according to its own favoured theories. Joan explained her visionary experiences in terms familiar to medieval Christianity. Subsequent commentators have interpreted them within the limits of their own understanding. George Bernard Shaw, writing in a sceptical age, brought his theory of the Life Force to bear on the saint's mysticism, and sought to disclose its significance for his contemporaries.

Brocken spectres observers standing on mountain peaks cast vast shadows on the surface of clouds below. These phenomena became known as Brocken spectres, taking the name from a mountain in Germany's Harz range

The Mere Iconography Does Not Matter

George Bernard Shaw notes that the world's main religions share a common conceptual apparatus for rendering the divine comprehensible to human intelligence. The world's vital forces are conceived as human figures. Teaching instils these figures in the mind of an individual, and in some cases that mind will project them as a physical reality. This is especially possible when the individual has practised austere living.

> The comparative study of religion became a refined discipline during the late nineteenth century, especially when the spread of European imperialism produced further encounters with non-European religious beliefs and systems of myth. George Bernard Shaw is keen to establish universal validity for his argument that Joan's hallucinations were imaginative projections of the Life Force, or manifestations of the 'evolutionary appetite'.

> Popular readiness to give credence to the existence of electromagnetism is invoked in order to show that faith in invisible forces is not merely the superstitious folly of an earlier age, but is equally relevant to the scientific mode of understanding.

The Modern Education which Joan Escaped

George Bernard Shaw notes the tension within modern education, initially affirming religious truth only to supplant it with the orthodoxies of modern science. He suggests that the Middle Ages possessed a set of beliefs which was better suited to its needs than that to which modern societies pledge allegiance: 'For us to set up our condition as a standard of sanity, and declare Joan mad because she never condescended to it, is to prove that we are not only lost but irredeemable' (p. 17).

George Bernard Shaw again stresses the practical value of visions, even for those who would use the authority of science to explain them away. He suggests that if Joan were born today she would receive the same basic training in Catholic belief, but it would be supplemented with seemingly incompatible awareness of recent developments in scientific knowledge. George Bernard Shaw suggests that the increased authority granted to science has resulted in a series of superstitious practices, which compare unfavourably to the more poetic aspects of religious faith. He is keen to counter accusations that Joan was insane; it is important to his presentation of her as an agent of evolutionary change that he shows her to have a heightened form of sanity, rather than being some freakishly abnormal figure. So, it serves his purpose to compare her to Florence Nightingale, a respected contemporary heroine.

Louis Pasteur (1822–95), French physician and microbiologist, who advocated inoculation against disease, and gave his name to pasteurisation, the process by which potentially harmful organisms are removed from milk

Paul Bert (1833–86), a French diplomat, who also specialised in physiology. He made important studies of the effects of air pressure upon the human body during such activities as diving and mountain-climbing

Galileo Galileo Galilei (1564–1642), Italian mathematician, physicist and astronomer, who championed the experimental method

the pre-Raphaelite movement group of English artists who in 1848 declared their intention to paint in the straightforward style which had flourished prior to the impact of the Italian painter Raphael (1483–1520)

Gadarene swine the pigs into which Jesus drove demoniac spirits, so they 'ran violently down a steep place into the sea'; see the New Testament, Matthew 8:28–33

Florence Nightingale (1820–1910), English nurse and reformer, who founded trained nursing as a profession for women

Failures of the Voices

George Bernard Shaw now argues that the voices and visions Joan heard were facets of an imaginative dramatisation, her way of 'finding out and making up her own mind' (p. 18).

> George Bernard Shaw continues to make a case for Joan as an eminently sane and practical individual. The saintly apparitions are cast in the light of stage props, enabling her to reach reasonable conclusions through imaginatively dramatic means.

> **Rationalism** philosophy which considers reason the sole means of acquiring knowledge, and which opposes faith in the supernatural or in divine revelation

Joan a Galtonic Visualizer

George Bernard Shaw identifies Joan as an example of what modern investigators of human psychology have called a 'visualizer'.

> The voices of Saints Catherine and Margaret, which Joan claimed to hear, were valuable to George Bernard Shaw to the extent that they conveyed practical wisdom. Her visions and voices were evidence of a highly imaginative faculty, developed within a medieval social and cultural context which accepted the authority of supernatural explanation. Here, George Bernard Shaw is explicitly casting Joan's visionary nature within the modern world's mode of understanding by invoking the scientific researches of Francis Galton. He refers to the perceptions of ordinary people as a way of indicating that the capacity for human evolution is not necessarily limited to a few extraordinary beings. He remarks that 'the street is full of normally sane people who have hallucinations of all sorts which they believe to be part of the normal permanent equipment of all human beings' (p. 19). It is worth noting that in a letter to the *New York Times*, written in June 1912, George Bernard Shaw described drama as 'sane hallucination'.

> **Francis Galton** (1822–1911) was an English explorer and anthropologist, knighted in 1909. He is remembered primarily for his studies of human intelligence, and for his advocacy of selective breeding to create superior

human beings. He coined the term 'eugenics' for this practice. George
Bernard Shaw found much he could agree with in eugenic theory. In his
book *Inquiries into Human Faculty and Its Development*, Francis Galton
noted that mentally healthy people can experience hallucinations as a result
of their intense ability to visualise

a magic lantern an early form of projector, using slides

Joan's Manliness and Militarism

Joan's father threatened to drown her if she tried to become a soldier.
That deterrent did not deflect her from the military life in later years.
George Bernard Shaw points out that Joan could have pursued her
mission on behalf of the Dauphin without assuming the conventional
trappings of masculinity. Envisaging that alternative, he draws
comparison with Queen Victoria. Joan, he concludes, was simply 'the sort
of woman that wants to lead a man's life' (p. 20).

After repudiating the abnormality of Joan's voices, George Bernard
Shaw turns to the other aspect of her character that has often been
taken as strange: her interest in 'soldiering and the masculine life'
(p. 19). Masculine and feminine domains had been clearly
demarcated for the middle classes of Victorian Britain. George
Bernard Shaw recognised that the early training of his initial
audiences would often have instilled clear-cut definitions along
gender lines, with women's place being securely in the home, while
adventuring was the province of men.

Queen Victoria, a figure looming still larger than Florence
Nightingale in the minds of George Bernard Shaw's
contemporaries, is invoked in order to draw a contrast between Joan
and a later woman who exercised power. Victoria, however,
retained women's clothing, and did not engage personally in the
warfare waged by her soldiers.

In order to remove Joan's taste for masculine apparel and conduct
from charges of abnormality, George Bernard Shaw refers to those
women who famously have disguised themselves as men, and have
entered service in the army or navy, escaping detection for a long
time. There are numerous traditional ballads which tell of such

adventures, but the organisation of modern armies scarcely allows for such concealments.

Noting in passing that the twentieth century has extended to women legal rights that were withheld in Victorian Britain, George Bernard Shaw points out that even during the nineteenth century there were many women who, while retaining feminine dress, assumed conventionally masculine responsibilities. In pre-Revolutionary Russia there were women soldiers, and he contests that it is only the need for women to reproduce that has more generally exempted them from military service.

to send Roberts to the Transvaal Frederick Sleigh Roberts (1832–1914), a respected field marshal, whose appointment as commander-in-chief of the British army during the South African war effectively brought to an end a series of damaging defeats

Rosa Bonheur (1822–99), a painter and sculptor, famous for detailed portrayal of animals. She lived unconventionally, and customarily wore trousers

George Sand the assumed name of Aurore Dudevant, née Dupin (1804–76), French novelist, renowned for her love affairs and unconventional lifestyle, including dressing as a man

her Chopins and De Mussets Frédéric Chopin (1810–49), Polish-French composer and pianist. Alfred de Musset (1810–57), French poet and playwright. Both men became lovers of George Sand

Was Joan Suicidal?

George Bernard Shaw denies accusations that Joan had suicidal tendencies, reiterating that 'There was nothing peculiar about her except the vigor and scope of her mind and character, and the intensity of her vital energy' (p. 20).

In order to show that Joan's apparent recklessness in the face of death was not a pathological state, George Bernard Shaw invokes two venerated British heroes of the war against Napoleon in the early nineteenth century: the Duke of Wellington and Lord Nelson.

He uses the anecdote concerning her escape from Beaurevoir Castle to show Joan's capacity to defy the voice of Saint Catherine, a fundamental independence of mind which he considered crucial to the historical role she assumed.

Joan Summed Up

Joan was 'a sane and shrewd country girl of extraordinary strength of mind and hardihood of body' (p. 21), a calculating rather than an impulsive woman, although the rapidity of her calculations gave the appearance of spontaneity. George Bernard Shaw is again emphatic that 'She was never for a moment what so many romancers and playwrights have pretended: a romantic young lady' (p. 21). Rather, she had the practical common sense of a respectable and rather prudish countrywoman. Her qualities made her, George Bernard Shaw suggests, 'a born boss' (p. 22).

> The importance George Bernard Shaw attached to his audience having an appropriate perception of Joan is evident from the emphatic repetitiveness of the Preface. He felt he had to clear away a considerable legacy of false information. In order to do so, the prefatory essay approaches Joan from a number of different angles, while insistently stressing those characteristics and qualities that made Joan, in his view, a highly relevant and significant figure for members of a modern audience. Napoleon and the Duke of Wellington feature here to help emphasise once more her practical abilities as a leader of men.
>
> Joan's tendency to prudishness is presented as a strategy for restoring self-respect to her forces. What might in other circumstances have been cast as a minor flaw in her character is portrayed as an effective means to a necessary end.
>
> **Jerichowise** alluding to Jericho, the town in Palestine whose walls, according to the Old Testament, fell at the sound of a trumpet blast

Joan's Immaturity and Ignorance

Imagining her as 'a managing woman of fifty' (p. 22), George Bernard Shaw reminds us that as Joan died while still in her teens, she had not acquired the skills of tact which come with experience. Her successes consequently came 'in the enterprises that were really simple and compassable by swift physical force' (p. 22). He notes her lack of academic education, and remarks that this left her incapable of tackling problems requiring scholarly understanding.

> George Bernard Shaw is pointing out that although Joan was a dynamic agent of human social evolution, she had limited awareness of the nature or extent of her role. In particular, she could not have been conscious that she was 'one of the precursors of a schism that rent Europe in two, and cost centuries of bloodshed that is not yet staunched' (p. 22): the conflict between Protestantism and the defenders of the Catholic faith. The perpetuation of that conflict was especially apparent to George Bernard Shaw, as an Irishman.

> An Irish perception of history seems also to inform his comment about Joan's objection to foreigners 'on the sensible ground that they were not in their proper place' (p. 22). A parallel is surely being implied between the English presence in Joan's France, and the British presence in twentieth-century Ireland.

> The dominant structures of religious and social organisation in the European Middle Ages were Catholicism and feudalism, 'both essentially international' (p. 22). National boundaries had limited significance in terms of how power was exercised. George Bernard Shaw points out that by adopting a view of life that was essentially Protestant and nationalist, Joan was going against the grain of her times in radical fashion, and was foreshadowing major historical changes.

The Maid in Literature

George Bernard Shaw considers characterisation of Joan in works by Shakespeare, Schiller, Voltaire, Mark Twain, Andrew Lang and Anatole France.

> In order to revise his audience's awareness of Joan as a historical figure, George Bernard Shaw saw the importance of reconsidering her representation in literature. In this section of the Preface, he

analyses the manner of her characterisation in earlier literary works, identifying more unwelcome lumber which needed to be cleared away.

George Bernard Shaw was not convinced that *Henry VI* was authentically the work of Shakespeare, and he regards the play's portrayal of Joan as comparable to the propagandist depictions in London newspapers of past and present enemies, such as George Washington, Napoleon, the German Crown Prince and Lenin. Consequently, it is a curiously mixed but utterly unsatisfactory depiction, with Joan in part romantic heroine, yet also sorceress or harlot.

In George Bernard Shaw's strategically dismissive view, Friedrich von Schiller's version was fully blown **romance**, managing to include 'not a single point of contact with the real Joan' (p. 23). Voltaire, on the other hand, used Joan merely as a vehicle for his ribald **satire** of contemporary institutions and fashions. George Bernard Shaw notes the importance of Jules Quicherat's publication of historical reports of the trial in removing Joan from the malleable domain of legend to the more resistant context of factual record. Quicherat, needless to say, was a primary source for George Bernard Shaw himself. He evaluates what he considers the less creditable use of that source by three other writers: Mark Twain, Andrew Lang and Anatole France.

Lenin Vladimir Ilyich Lenin (1870–1924), militant Marxist who founded the Russian Communist Party, led the Bolshevik Revolution, and became principal architect of the Soviet state

Schiller Friedrich von Schiller (1759–1805), German dramatist, poet and literary theorist, whose work was generally concerned with the need to rise above material constraints. He wrote of Joan in *Die Jungfrau von Orleans* (1801)

Voltaire pseudonym of François-Marie Arouet (1694–1778), satirical writer, who relentlessly opposed tyranny and attacked bigotry in all its guises, especially religious prejudice. He wrote of Joan in his poem, *La Pucelle* (*c*.1755)

Homer legendary Greek poet (*c*. eighth century BC), author of two epics: the *Iliad* and the *Odyssey*

Pecksniffian a slimy hypocrite, after Pecksniff in *Martin Chuzzlewit* (1844), a novel by Charles Dickens (1812–70)

Samuel Butler (1835–1902), English novelist and critic, whose **satire** *Erewhon* (1872) addressed religion and evolution in terms that reflected the decline of the Victorian faith in inevitable and irreversible progress

Agnes Sorel (1422–50), mistress of Charles VII of France. Accounts suggesting that she continued the work of Joan by inspiring the king to action and by surrounding him with sagacious advisers have been discredited

écraser l'infâme literally, 'destroy the infamous thing', expressing concisely Voltaire's vehement opposition to the Church

Quicherat Jules Quicherat (1814–82), French historian and archaeologist. His transcription of the trial of 1431, and of the rehabilitation proceedings of 1456 were published in five volumes (1841–9), and were translated into English by T. Douglas Murray, in 1902, as *Jeanne d'Arc, Maid of Orleans, Deliverer of France: Being the Story of Her Life, Her Achievements and Her Death, as Attested on Oath and Set Forth in the Original Documents*

Mark Twain pseudonym of Samuel Langhorne Clemens (1835–1910), American novelist and satirical humorist, author of *Personal Recollections of Joan of Arc* (1896)

Andrew Lang (1844–1912), Scottish scholar, noted for collections of fairy-tales, and translations of Homer, and author of *Maid of France* (1908)

Anatole France (1844–1924), erudite French novelist and critic, awarded the Nobel Prize for literature in 1921. He assumed a sceptical point of view in his *La Vie de Jeanne d'Arc* (1908)

Bayard (1475–1524), a French knight, who attained heroic status during Charles VII's campaign in Italy

Esther Summerson from Bleak House gentle heroine in the novel by Charles Dickens, published in 1853

Protestant Misunderstandings of the Middle Ages

George Bernard Shaw contends that proper understanding of Joan's story requires a grasp of context as well as character. An accurate sense of the realities of the Catholic Middle Ages is needed, and neither the American Mark Twain nor the Scot Andrew Lang possessed this.

George Bernard Shaw seeks to establish Joan's relevance to contemporary audiences, not by concealing differences between their own experiences and those of people living during the Middle Ages, but by highlighting the need to be responsive to one's time, as Joan was to her own. Importantly, this might mean adopting a set of attitudes very different to those prevailing in society, and involve being prepared to engage in controversy.

George Bernard Shaw is establishing here a basis for his case against the view that Peter Cauchon and his fellow adjudicators were merely vicious in their treatment of Joan. It is important to his purpose that Joan's story should not be framed as good versus evil, but should be seen as part of a more complex historical process.

A Yankee at the Court of King Arthur *A Connecticut Yankee in King Arthur's Court*, a novel by Mark Twain published in 1889
Walter Scott (1771–1832), an influential and popular author of historical novels, often set in the Middle Ages
Albigensians members of a Christian sect, originating in the south of France, which denounced the Church as corrupt. Persecuted as heretics throughout the twelfth and thirteenth centuries, the Albigensians were eventually eradicated by the Inquisition

Comparative Fairness of Joan's Trial

George Bernard Shaw defends Joan's judge, Bishop Peter Cauchon, against charges of bigotry.

The process of salvaging Cauchon's reputation continues. George Bernard Shaw's characterisation in the play presents the bishop as essentially fair and just, and he seeks to vindicate that view in his Preface. He alludes to comparable contemporary cases, the trials of Edith Cavell and Roger Casement. The latter was particularly relevant to George Bernard Shaw, who wrote a speech read to the court by Casement, following the decision that he should be executed (see Historical Background – Irish Nationalism). The medieval Catholic court is compared favourably to the modern military 'Inquisition' that condemned Cavell. George Bernard

Shaw takes the opportunity to suggest hypocrisy and cynical opportunism in the posthumous favour shown Cavell by the British authorities, who had disparaged during her lifetime her readiness to nurse enemy soldiers. He pointedly omits further reference to Casement here, but uses the Cavell case to accuse the British establishment of moral cowardice.

George Bernard Shaw is basically arguing that what is often taken to be progress in historical terms is cosmetic window-dressing, rather than the genuinely evolutionary advance that interests him. He claims that in practice modern Londoners show no more tolerance than the officials of Rouen who executed Joan in 1431.

Edith Cavell (1865–1915), English nurse, a popular heroine of the First World War, executed by Germany for her role in assisting Allied soldiers to escape from occupied Belgium

Roger Casement (1864–1916), an Irish-born diplomat who performed high-level public service for the British, but was eventually executed as a traitor. During the First World War, he unsuccessfully sought German assistance for the Irish cause, and, despite protests from influential public figures, he was hanged in London

Tommy and Jerry and Pitou the *poilu* popular names for British, German and French soldiers

Miss Sylvia Pankhurst (1882–1960), like her mother Emmeline a leading member of the British suffragist movement, which campaigned to have the right to vote extended to women

the Peculiar People a Christian sect devoted to faith healing, founded in London in 1838

Joan Not Tried as a Political Offender

George Bernard Shaw contrasts the 'national political trial' of Casement with the universal ecclesiastical judgement that condemned Joan for heresy. The simple, sensual and emotional nature of Joan's piety is contrasted with the complex, formal and intellectual foundation of Cauchon's faith. George Bernard Shaw then calls into question the validity of Joan's politically convenient rehabilitation, twenty-five years after her death.

Although Joan's nationalism is recognised as a threat by the Earl of Warwick, heresy provided the actual grounds for her trial. The nature of her faith did not conform to the institutional religion of her day, although the strength of her belief was beyond dispute. In drawing out the difference between Joan's form of Christian faith and that of Cauchon, George Bernard Shaw is not only consolidating his defence of the bishop as a reasonable man, but also furthering his case that Joan was the first Protestant. He suggests that Mark Twain's and Andrew Lang's modern Protestant versions of Joan displayed an ignorance of the doctrinal law of the medieval Church comparable to their ignorance of Joan herself.

Proceedings were held twenty-five years after her execution, ostensibly to redress the wrong committed in her burning. George Bernard Shaw seeks to disclose an act of cynical opportunism through reference to another inversion of reputation. When he died in 1658, Oliver Cromwell was buried as a hero, but in 1660, following the Restoration of the monarchy, his body was exhumed and hung from Tyburn gallows. George Bernard Shaw contrasts this posthumous condemnation with Joan's posthumous rehabilitation. The real motivation for rehabilitation was that Charles VII, the French king, could not be seen to owe his position to the actions of a heretical sorceress. Popular support in France for the Maid of Orleans, who had precipitated the departure of the English, meant there was widespread approval for this challenge to the Church's authority.

the Burgundian faction the feudal nobility of Burgundy entered into an alliance with the English invaders
Wycliffe John Wycliffe (*c.*1330–84), English religious reformer, a precursor in his beliefs of the Protestant Reformation
Mrs Eddy Mary Baker Eddy (1821–1910), an American who founded the faith known as Christian Science

The Church Uncompromised by its Amends

Protestantism differs from Catholicism in the emphasis it places upon private judgement. But verified personal experience of direct revelation from God is one of the defining criteria for sainthood within the Catholic Church. The saint's 'private judgment is privileged' (p. 29). According to this argument, a very thin line exists between saintliness and heresy, and a reversal of judgement, such as that which led to Joan's rehabilitation, appears perfectly feasible.

> Although George Bernard Shaw condemns the burning of Joan, he wishes to show that Cauchon was acting not out of petty malice, but in accordance with the understanding of justice espoused by the institution he represented. Defence of Cauchon is crucial to George Bernard Shaw's insistence that a clash of differing world-views, rather than a conflict of heroes and villains, lies at the heart of Joan's story. To ensure that the bishop is seen as a man acting in good faith, George Bernard Shaw needs to defend the integrity of the Catholic Church in the face of the subsequent inversion undergone by its judgement in this case.

> **Clare** Saint Clare (1194–1253), from Assisi, was inspired by Saint Francis to form the order known as 'Poor Clares', embracing a life of poverty. She was canonised in 1255
>
> ***Tout comprendre, c'est tout pardonner*** literally, 'To understand all is to forgive all'
>
> **the Marquesas islanders** inhabitants of volcanic islands in the South Pacific

Cruelty, Modern and Medieval

George Bernard Shaw discusses relatively recent instances of cruel execution, and observes, 'We are still flogging criminals, and clamoring for more flogging' (p. 31). He criticises the inhumanity of modern prisons. In conclusion, he argues that the Church would have followed a wiser path in excommunicating Joan, rather than condemning her to the choice between prison or death.

> The Preface is a concerted attempt to demystify Joan's story, and to make the participants in it appear explicable human beings, rather than freaks of supernatural vision or of superhuman cruelty. George Bernard Shaw remarks that Joan's burning was not an exceptional form of execution, any more than the crucifixion of Christ. They

shared the common fate of transgressors in their own and later times.

Shifting his focus slightly, George Bernard Shaw launches a brief attack on the inhumanity of the modern penal system. His friends and fellow Fabians, Sidney and Beatrice Webb had recently published a study of conditions in English prisons, and he adds to their criticism of the debasing effects of the system. Joan chose to go to the stake rather than face a life of close confinement. As ever, George Bernard Shaw is concerned to make this detail relevant to modern understanding.

Sidney and Beatrice Webb Sidney Webb (1859–1947) and his wife Beatrice Webb (1858–1943), distinguished historians and pioneers of social reform, were early members of the Fabian Society and were co-founders of the London School of Economics and Political Science

Richard Wagner (1813–83), a German composer whose operas changed the course of European musical history

primitive Calibanism (in Browning's sense) the poem 'Caliban upon Setebos' (1855) by Robert Browning (1812–89) is an expression of the crude thinking of Caliban, the bestial figure from Shakespeare's *The Tempest*

Catholic Anti-Clericalism

George Bernard Shaw suggests that the great reforming moments within Catholicism have sprung from dissatisfaction with the conduct of the established clergy. Joan was unequivocal in her rejection of the authority of the priesthood.

Once more, George Bernard Shaw is keen to show that Joan was extraordinary in degree, in level of intensity, rather than in kind. Dissatisfaction with priests has by no means been uncommon within the history of the Catholic Church. Joan's feelings were not unprecedented, but she went further in her rebelliousness, and so may be seen to have initiated Protestantism.

Laodiceanism indifference to matters of religion, as exemplified by the people of Laodicea, mentioned in Revelation 3:14–18

Ulster Orangeman a member of the Orange Society, an association of Protestants established in Ireland in 1795 to defend their faith and the legacy of William III, Prince of Orange

Leicester Low Church Robert Dudley, Earl of Leicester (*c*.1533–88), a favourite courtier of Elizabeth I, was a Puritan who led the Protestant persecution of Roman Catholics in Britain. Low Church refers to his followers

Henry Nevinson (d.1941), English journalist and war correspondent

Gallio (c. 5BC–AD65), Roman official who dismissed charges made against Saint Paul by the Jews

Machiavelli Niccolò Machiavelli (1469–1527), Florentine statesman, author of *The Prince*, a treatise of political philosophy. His name has become associated with the expedient view that the end justifies the means

Rubicon a small river which once formed the boundary between Roman Italy and Cisalpine Gaul, a province overseen by Julius Caesar. Crossing the Rubicon, he effectively declared war on the Roman Republic, so the term has come to signify an irrevocable decision

Catholicism Not Yet Catholic Enough

George Bernard Shaw argues that Churches must learn humility in order to acknowledge that persons of genius can attain enlightened understanding in advance of institutions. Otherwise, acts of overt persecution occur, as in the cases of Joan, Giordano Bruno and Galileo.

In his own favoured terms, George Bernard Shaw's point is that human institutions should be responsive to the Life Force which may be channelled through individuals. Once the institutions become rigidly unreceptive, vital development is stifled.

the Apostolic Succession the transmission through bishops of spiritual authority derived from Christ's disciples

the Church Militant Christians on Earth

Bruno Giordano Bruno (1548–1600), Italian philosopher, astronomer and mathematician. His unorthodox views on the nature of the universe anticipated modern scientific views, but he died at the stake on account of them

The Law of Change is the Law of God

George Bernard Shaw notes that the Church does not operate through 'deification of the democratic average', rather it is a hierarchic structure, with the Pope at its head. It is unsatisfactory, he suggests, because 'selection and election are of the superior by the inferior', a process which he identifies as 'the cardinal vice of democracy' (p. 33). Consequently, there have been few great popes, and those who have existed have been the product of accident rather than of conscious design.

> George Bernard Shaw's argument is that the self-selected, like Joan, are the authentic leaders of human society. In elections, such as those which choose a new pope, voters seek to appoint someone who will best serve their own self-centred and short-sighted interests. George Bernard Shaw's premise is fundamentally undemocratic, and helps explain why he was able on occasion to voice support for totalitarian regimes. He knew that some would find his point of view unpalatable, but took that as proof of its validity, for 'all evolution in thought and conduct must at first appear as heresy and misconduct' (p. 34).
>
> Joan is here brought unequivocally into line with George Bernard Shaw's theories of the Life Force and of Creative Evolution, expounded in the plays *Man and Superman* and *Back to Methuselah* (see Theme on Creative Evolution and the Life Force).
>
> **Ibsen** Henrik Ibsen (1828–1906), Norwegian playwright, greatly admired by George Bernard Shaw, who wrote the first study in English of his work

Credulity, Modern and Medieval

George Bernard Shaw laments the coercive practices of the Church. He notes how doctors of medicine have assumed something of the role of priests, and some of their power to dictate behaviour.

> George Bernard Shaw is anxious that readers should not perceive coercion through faith to be exclusively a thing of the past. He cites contemporary medical practitioners as equivalent to the priesthood, and argues that faith in doctors is actually more susceptible to

unscrupulous manipulation. We should remember that he was writing in the days before the National Health Service, when doctors had a vested financial interest which priests usually did not have.

Abernethy John Abernethy (1764–1831), renowned English surgeon
Archbishop Laud William Laud (1573–1645), an influential statesman under Charles I and Archbishop of Canterbury from 1633 until his execution under Oliver Cromwell

Toleration, Modern and Medieval

What if Joan had been excommunicated, but not executed? George Bernard Shaw speculates that she might have founded her own Church. He then compares the medieval Catholic Church's intolerance with the regulations imposed in order to ensure modern hygiene in sanitation, and concludes: 'We must face the fact that society is founded on intolerance' (p. 35).

George Bernard Shaw's use of the word 'prate' is noteworthy; it is usually used when the speaker is a child, so in this discussion of religion and scientific medicine it has particular resonance, implying the functioning of a childlike dependency within democratic societies. That, and his suggestion that intolerance is invariably the basis of social coherence, highlight once more the pronounced strand of illiberal, fundamentally anti-democratic sentiment in George Bernard Shaw's thinking.

Consider the extreme declaration that 'We must persecute, even to the death' (p. 36). George Bernard Shaw was a socialist, but, unlike a Marxist, who would invest responsibility for historical change in a class of people, George Bernard Shaw took the view that unconventional individuals were the agents of change, a view partly based on his reading of the German philosopher, Friedrich Nietzsche (1844–1900). The preservation of social order always necessitates some form of persecution, he argues, but the danger is that sages will be mistaken for lunatics, and saviours for blasphemers. In order to minimise the danger of such damaging error, he argues for 'a large liberty to shock conventional people', in order to promote 'the value of originality, individuality, and eccentricity' (p. 36).

the Bulls of Pope Leo Pope Leo X (1513–21) issued an edict which excommunicated Martin Luther

Butler's Erewhon satire published in 1872 by Samuel Butler (see above)

Sanitarians member of a group advocating hygienic reforms

Variability of Toleration

Degrees of toleration vary according to circumstances, with measures being taken during times of war which would be otherwise unthinkable.

George Bernard Shaw makes another political point about the British presence in Ireland. More generally, he is arguing that toleration is not an absolute quality, but depends upon social and historical context. The nineteenth century had no justification for supposing itself more tolerant in practice than the fifteenth. The Inquisition has modern equivalents. George Bernard Shaw insists that Bishop Cauchon was far more scrupulous in conducting the trial than a twentieth-century judge might be. In George Bernard Shaw's diagnosis there remained many things wrong with modern European capitalist society. As a committed socialist, he was keen to counter any complacent sense that significant change was no longer a historical necessity.

the Fascisti armed gangs who exercised a reign of terror in Mussolini's Italy in the early 1920s

the Black and Tans a British auxiliary police force, notorious for its ferocity, deployed between July 1920 and July 1921 to counter republican rebellion in Ireland. The name was derived from a distinctive uniform

Star Chamber an ancient court of civil and criminal jurisdiction, renowned for its abuse of power. It was abolished in 1641

the Habeas Corpus Act Act of Parliament, passed in 1679, designed to preclude unlawful imprisonment

a Defence of The Realm Act a series of Acts of Parliament passed during the First World War, granting absolute authority to the government of the day in matters of national security

The Conflict Between Genius and Discipline

Government, in its various forms, depends upon the willingness of people to follow orders. Joan created enemies largely through her insistence on giving orders to those who would have considered themselves to have authority over her, and would have expected her to adopt a subservient position of obedience. She assumed authority by claiming that God spoke through her.

> Bringing 'the matter home to ourselves' (p. 37) is George Bernard Shaw's crucial concern in this Preface. His doubts about current democratic government can be seen clearly here, once again, as he argues that most people are happy to obey orders, rather than being obliged to think for themselves. He stresses the importance of prevailing social conditions in shaping our readiness to obey.

Joan as Theocrat

Joan's claim to speak for God led to clear-cut divisions between those who followed her ardently as a consequence, and those who condemned her as a heretic or a witch. In more mundane terms, those who recognised her callowness and consequently mistrusted her ability to lead were appalled at the popular credulity that placed her temporarily in a position of real power.

> George Bernard Shaw seeks to remove Joan's case from the specific medieval context of belief in witches and angels, in order to disclose eminently practical and reasonable grounds for the opposition to her.

Unbroken Success Essential in Theocracy

George Bernard Shaw considers the historical reasons for Joan's failure to forge 'an unbroken chain of overwhelming successes in the military and political field' (p. 39).

> A theocratic society is one governed under the direction of God. Medieval Europe was, in effect, such a society. George Bernard Shaw points out that for Joan to convince those in power that she represented the authority of God, she had to be consistently

successful in her actions. Any flaws in her performance as leader would be taken to contradict her claims.

George Bernard Shaw shifts his focus on to the historical realities of Joan's military career, the actual context within which her contemporaries had to judge the validity of her claim to a privileged relationship with God's truth. The more recent case of Garibaldi is cited as a possible parallel in order to bring the story closer to home.

Garibaldi Giuseppe Garibaldi (1807–82), Italian patriot and soldier, who played a major part in the process of unifying Italy under the house of Savoy

Modern Distortions of Joan's History

George Bernard Shaw's attention turns back from the prosaic historical version of Joan to the character bearing her name who has featured in the **melodramatic** legend of the 'wicked bishop and the ensnared maiden' (p. 39).

George Bernard Shaw's sense that ends may justify means informs this Preface, and with reference to familiar accounts of Joan's story, he declares, 'It would be far less misleading if they were wrong as to the facts, and right in their view of the facts' (p. 39). He suggests that a kind of mental straitjacket restricts understanding, so 'it is difficult, if not impossible, for most people to think otherwise than in the fashion of their own period' (p. 40). The observation contrasts the limitations of the majority with Joan's visionary awareness.

History Always Out of Date

George Bernard Shaw remarks that schoolchildren are taught past history, but are fed lies about the unfolding present. Once a safe distance has been reached, the catalytic figures of history are incorporated into the record, although Joan has suffered through being reviled by both Protestant and Catholic historians.

In his play, George Bernard Shaw is seeking to provide an alternative to familiar historical accounts of Joan. *Saint Joan* is intended to entertain, but at moments in the Preface such as this, we are in no doubt as to George Bernard Shaw's serious, educative purpose. The Preface is clearing away the debris of previous interpretations, so the play can serve up the truth 'without any sauce at all' (p. 40).

Clearly, throughout the prefatory essay, the tense political situation in Ireland was never far from George Bernard Shaw's thoughts.

The Real Joan Not Marvellous Enough for Us

George Bernard Shaw observes that modern life does not allow the kind of faith that Joan had, and which she required from her followers. It does nonetheless have a host of 'marvel mongers', not least in the scientific community (p. 40).

> Satirising both faddist occultism, and the forms of belief demanded by those experts who legislate modern science, George Bernard Shaw **ironically** declares that he is defending his own age against the charge that it is less imaginative than the Middle Ages. Modern physics has moved into a world beyond direct sensory perception, and we are required to give credence to more that is marvellous than were our medieval ancestors. Belief in the existence of electrons requires no less credulousness on our part than belief in angels did for the Middle Ages. Still being ironic, he contends that reluctance to accept that Joan was a witch shows that our taste for marvels is greater than that of our predecessors, not less. She was not sufficiently spectacular for us. George Bernard Shaw is again disparaging claims made for the more enlightened condition of modernity.

Betelgeuse star in the constellation Orion that appears to be deep red and is one of the brightest features of the night sky

The Stage Limits of Historical Representation

The playwright affirms that his play contains 'all that need be known' about Joan, even though he has had to condense her life into a three-and-a-half-hour span (p. 41). He explains that his characterisation of the supporting cast is guided by practical considerations, aiming for a suitable effect rather than aspiring to accuracy that is unattainable because of inadequate documentation.

George Bernard Shaw requires audiences to recognise the essential truth of his representation of Joan, even though the stage necessitates artifice through its constraints of space and time. His pragmatic approach to characterisation of the other figures in the play is a relatively innocuous instance of his view that valid ends may justify questionable means.

He remarks, almost incidentally, that 'a man always describes himself unconsciously whenever he describes anyone else' (p. 42). It is hard for us, reading this, not to conclude that his description of Joan is actually telling us a great deal about George Bernard Shaw. He formed a complex identification with her, as an agent of the Life Force, and had a statuette of the saint erected in his garden.

> **the Uffizi in Florence** the Uffizi Gallery is a famous art museum in Florence, renowned especially for its collection of Italian Renaissance painting

A Void in the Elizabethan Drama

George Bernard Shaw expresses indebtedness to nineteenth-century rediscovery of the Middle Ages, following centuries in which they were seen through the distorting lens offered by the Renaissance. Shakespeare's plays did not generate the authentic atmosphere of the Catholic Middle Ages; his characters were Protestant in their individualism, scepticism and self-centredness. George Bernard Shaw's own play portrays 'the Church, the Inquisition, the Feudal System, with divine inspiration always beating against their too inelastic limits' (p. 43).

> George Bernard Shaw is boldly critical of Shakespeare; that in itself is a highly significant gesture against authority for a literary man to make. He objects to the absence from Shakespearean drama of any sense that 'the world is finally governed by forces expressing themselves in religions and laws which make epochs rather than by vulgarly ambitious individuals who make rows' (p. 42). George Bernard Shaw accuses Shakespeare of being too narrowly fixed in his sense that individuals should be self-regulating, a conception alien to medieval Catholicism. George Bernard Shaw suggests that this explains much of Shakespeare's appeal for the English middle

classes, who cherish self-interest and are generally oblivious to the larger requirements of the social system.

the King Maker Richard Neville, First Earl of Warwick (1428–71) became known as 'the King Maker' during the Wars of the Roses. He obtained power for Edward IV in 1461, and secured the restoration of Henry VI ten years later

Tragedy, Not Melodrama

George Bernard Shaw explains that his play is not about crime and punishment, but is essentially concerned with 'what normally innocent people do'. He argues that murders committed with pious intentions, as was the case with Joan's execution, introduce a comic element of contradiction into the tragedy of death. As he puts it, 'the angels may weep at the murder, but the gods laugh at the murderers' (p. 43).

It has been evident all along that George Bernard Shaw has been determined to counter any suggestion that his play is simply a conflict of good and evil. Now, he makes explicit his position that while depiction of villainy results in **melodrama**, his approach to characterisation should be seen to produce high tragedy.

diabolus ex machina literally, a devil out of the machine
deus ex machina literally, a god out of the machine. The phrase usually refers to theatrical contrivance designed to resolve a dramatic plot

The Inevitable Flatteries of Tragedy

George Bernard Shaw states explicitly that 'the writer of high tragedy and comedy, aiming at the innermost attainable truth, must needs flatter Cauchon nearly as much as the melodramatist vilifies him' (p. 44). Yet historical evidence shows the bishop to have been neither a scoundrel nor a paragon. The playwright's Cauchon and Lemaître must make intelligible the Church and the Inquisition. His Warwick must elucidate for modern audiences the feudal system of social organisation.

George Bernard Shaw returns to his earlier point about people in a particular age lacking the ability to articulate what is peculiar to their time, its salient qualities. Such awareness, he argues, is feasible in dramatic representation, and so he has striven to make key characters say 'the things they actually would have said if they had known what they were really doing' (p. 44). Dramatic characterisation allows a degree of distortion which effectively lifts figures out of their immersion in events and enables them to give voice to their role in the unfolding history of their time.

Some Well-meant Proposals for the Improvement of the Play

George Bernard Shaw considers the reception of his play in America and in England, and, with **ironic** thanks for their suggestions, summarily dismisses critics whose recommendations would remove not only the Epilogue, but also 'all the references to such undramatic and tedious matters as the Church, the feudal system, the Inquisition, the theory of heresy and so forth' (pp. 44–5).

> George Bernard Shaw makes fun of those theatre critics who have presumed to offer him advice on stagecraft. He says that they would edit out all that was really important in the play, in order to make room for decorative ornamentation and shallow artifice.
>
> His reference to members of the audience missing their trains was aimed at a specific target. The play's American producers initially demanded cuts in order to ensure *Saint Joan* finished early enough to allow easy train travel. George Bernard Shaw refused to comply, so the production had to be scheduled earlier in the evening. He refused to compromise the artistic integrity of the play for the convenience of playgoers.
>
> **Mr Matheson Lang** (1879–1948), English romantic actor and dramatist, who in 1914 inaugurated the Shakespeare seasons at London's Old Vic theatre
> **The Wandering Jew** in Christian legend, a figure doomed to wander until the end of the world, because he taunted Christ on his way to the crucifixion

The Epilogue

George Bernard Shaw defends inclusion of his epilogue as a necessary means to show 'the canonized Joan as well as the incinerated one' (p. 45).

The Epilogue has attracted more adverse criticism than any other part of the play. Some critics have argued that it is superfluous, but George Bernard Shaw is adamant that the execution needs to be seen as the beginning of the story, not its conclusion. That end justifies the Epilogue as a means. George Bernard Shaw's argument seems to suggest, although it remains unstated, a parallel between Joan and Jesus Christ, whose real work in the world began after His crucifixion.

To the Critics, Lest They Should Feel Ignored

George Bernard Shaw discusses the lot of the theatre critic and the nature of the standard audience. He accuses both of hypocrisy, suggesting that nine-tenths of criticism in the press is essentially saying, 'I cannot associate pleasure with any sort of intellectual activity; and I dont believe anyone else can either' (p. 46). Defiantly, he proclaims that he writes drama in the classical manner, for those who have the capacity and the will to appreciate it.

George Bernard Shaw's attention has now moved exclusively to the conditions of performance for a contemporary play, the competing pressures exerted by paying audience and paid critic. His attitude is broadly cynical, and he suggests that many theatregoers attend for any reason other than 'interest in dramatic art as such' (p. 46). Complaints about missing trains home are cited as examples of philistinism, characteristic of critics incapable of grasping the real quality of George Bernard Shaw's classical comedies and tragedies. He did not write for the fashion-conscious dilettante.

George Bernard Shaw explains his indifference to such criticism by comparison with the physicist Albert Einstein's indifference to people baffled by mathematics. Just as Joan is compared to Napoleon, so the playwright is prepared to compare himself to a recognised genius in another field.

Surrey or Middlesex George Bernard Shaw is probably alluding to the Oval and Lord's, cricket grounds and homes to the sides representing these English counties. Spectators prepared to spend an entire day watching the

game would probably resist an invitation to invest equal time in attending
the performance of a play
Ober-Ammergau village in the Bavarian Alps which has staged a lengthy
Passion play every ten years since 1634

SCENE I   **Joan visits Robert de Baudricourt, and persuades him to
grant assistance for her mission to lift the siege of Orleans
and to see the Dauphin crowned**

It is a fine spring morning in 1429. In a chamber of the castle of
Vaucouleurs, Captain Robert de Baudricourt, the castle's squire, berates
his cowering steward because there are no eggs. The steward protests that
the hens will not lay, and adds that the cows are no longer giving milk.
He asserts that the countryside has been bewitched, and lays blame
specifically on the Maid from Domrémy (Joan of Arc). The Maid has
been at Vaucouleurs for two days, and refuses to leave. She lingers in the
courtyard, talking to the soldiers, and praying. Her 'positive' manner has
intimidated the steward; he understands that she wishes to be a soldier.
The squire summons her to the chamber.

She is a country girl in her late teens. On arrival, she demands from
Baudricourt a horse and armour, and his approval for her mission to
secure the coronation of the Dauphin. She insists he should comply
because these orders come from her Lord, the King of Heaven. The
squire immediately declares that she is mad. She responds that this is a
common reaction, which will be dispelled once he recognises that she is
following the will of God, and she asks for three soldiers to help her raise
the siege of Orleans.

De Baudricourt is outraged that Joan calls squire Bertrand de
Poulengey 'Polly', and knows John of Metz as Jack. He is overwhelmed
by her impudence, but she counters his condescension by asserting that
his passage to Paradise is assured, through the agency of Saint Catherine
and Saint Margaret who speak to her daily. The girl is dismissed to the
courtyard, and de Poulengey is summoned to the chamber.

De Baudricourt advises de Poulengey not to become too closely
involved with the Maid. 'Polly' replies that the girl has a mysterious
quality, which has won his respect and that of the common soldiers. He
argues that his countrymen require a miracle to halt the spreading power

of the English king, who has already taken Paris and effectively controls the castle in which they stand. The Dauphin, who should rule France, is weak and ineffectual. Joan, a potential miracle-worker, seems to offer a positive alternative.

De Baudricourt wavers, and eventually succumbs to de Poulengey's display of commitment to the Maid's cause. Joan is recalled, and he asks her about herself, and about her visions of Saint Catherine and Saint Margaret. She refuses to disclose details of the visions, but reiterates her mission to drive the English from France and to crown the Dauphin in Rheims Cathedral. She insists that with God on their side her soldiers will win; it is only pettiness that hinders troops. They will succeed once they realise that they are agents of God's will. The squire accedes to her demands and sends her to the Dauphin in Chinon. After her departure, he acknowledges that there is 'something about her' (p. 62). The steward enters excitedly, carrying a basket of newly laid eggs. The formerly sceptical squire is startled, and takes this as a sign that Joan has indeed 'come from God' (p. 62).

> De Baudricourt asks his steward if he takes him for a cowboy, by which he means, literally, a boy who tends cattle. The steward acknowledges that on the contrary the squire is more powerful than the king himself. This may appear an exaggeration, but it does reflect accurately the status of a feudal lord during the European Middle Ages. George Bernard Shaw was keen that the realities of that feudal society should permeate his play.

> Importantly, however, the characterisation of de Baudricourt, initially abusive and bullying, discloses personal failings, which seem inappropriate to his elevated status. Joan's strength is focused in her capacity to be 'positive'. His underlying lack of will-power is contrasted with Joan's confident assertiveness. De Baudricourt's lack of will also foreshadows the more pronounced feebleness of the Dauphin.

> The steward tells his squire, 'we are afraid of you; but she puts courage into us' (p. 51). One of the main points George Bernard Shaw is making in this play is that power rarely resides with those best suited to wield it; no more in modern democracies

than in feudal societies are leaders, usually, the best people to promote beneficial change and advance the evolution of human societies.

George Bernard Shaw discloses a readiness amongst people in fifteenth-century Europe to accredit any unusual occurrence to witchcraft. At the same time, he indicates that these events might have a very mundane character, such as a dearth of eggs and milk. These might now be explained in perfectly rational terms, but, as he argues in his Preface, we should not be blind in modern times to our own gullibility and capacity for superstitious belief.

De Baudricourt's reference to burning witches anticipates the unfolding of Joan's story, and signals that such an execution was by no means a rare event. George Bernard Shaw wants Joan to be seen as extraordinary only in her openness to the Life Force; she must not be seen as a freak, or a character from **romance**. Receptiveness is the crucial factor, so, as Joan realises, if troops act as conscious agents of God they will be capable of feats inconceivable to mere fighting men. George Bernard Shaw substituted Life Force for God in his beliefs, but the point remained that individuals could rise above their apparent limitations if open to this greater influence.

When de Poulengey is describing the effect Joan has had upon him he announces that 'Her words and her ardent faith in God have put fire into me' (p. 57). Such allusion to fire, unconscious of its eventual relevance to Joan's fate, is **ironic**. He also declares, 'We want a few mad people now. See where the sane ones have landed us!' (p. 57). In George Bernard Shaw's day, this kind of desperate logic was quite common amongst protesters against the horrors of the First World War. For example, the movement known as Dada created deliberately nonsensical art in order to challenge the claims and presuppositions of a civilisation built on common sense.

Lorraine is referred to as a territory distinct from France, although they share a language. Modern notions of national unity and identity were not then in place. The ruling class generally felt affinities amongst their own kind, across geographical boundaries, to be stronger than any bond with the lower classes of their own lands (see Historical Background – The Feudal System). George Bernard Shaw presents Joan as the first nationalist, refusing to be constrained by class demarcations, and promoting the interests of France, defined as the country where French was spoken. De Baudricourt, as a feudal lord, considers language an irrelevance; it becomes a crucial factor only with the emergence of the modern conception of nationhood.

Joan objects to the English on the grounds that they belong elsewhere and speak another language. The issue had special relevance to George Bernard Shaw's native Ireland, where the occupying English had suppressed the indigenous language and imposed their own, as part of the process of colonisation. Allusion to the brutality of English soldiers is surely also intended to reflect the colonial history of Ireland. George Bernard Shaw refers in the Preface to the notorious, and then recent, activity of the Black and Tans.

Joan speaks a distinctive form of regional English; her eccentric grammar ('Be you captain?'), in particular, contrasts with the more standardised mode of speech used by the ruling-class characters in the play (see Language and Style). As her father's lord, the squire was responsible for her protection. In such details, George Bernard Shaw is indicating the different set of social relations that existed within feudal society. Yet de Baudricourt asserts that she is a bourgeoise, a member of a middle class which had no real social importance at that time. Application of the term 'bourgeoise', coined much later, is an instance of George Bernard Shaw's use of **anachronism** to make medieval action relevant to modern audiences (See Dramatic Technique and Structure – Anachronism).

Saint Denis the patron saint of France
the Black Prince Edward, Prince of Wales (1330–76), eldest son of the English king, Edward III. In 1356 his troops defeated the French at Poitiers in one of the most famous battles of the Hundred Years War

SCENE II   **Joan is granted an audience with the Dauphin and his court. Despite opposition from some of the courtiers, she is granted command of the army**

It is 8 March 1429, late in the afternoon. In a curtained-off section of the throne room in the castle of Chinon, in Lorraine, the Archbishop of Rheims and Monseigneur de la Trémouille, the Lord Chamberlain, await the arrival of the Dauphin. The archbishop's composure contrasts with the brooding impatience of Trémouille. They have divergent attitudes, but both men are owed money by the Dauphin, and are mystified that he has spent so much with so little to show for it.

A page announces the arrival of Gilles de Rais, known as Bluebeard on account of his small beard, curled and dyed. Bluebeard brings news of Foul Mouthed Frank, an inveterate swearer, who was warned by a soldier to desist from cursing as his death was imminent. Soon afterwards he fell into a well and drowned. Captain La Hire, a hardened fighter, enters. He also is renowned for swearing, and, as Bluebeard has intimated, he is now fraught with anxiety. La Hire asserts that the soldier who delivered the warning was actually an angel in disguise.

The Dauphin, the uncrowned King Charles VII, enters. He is physically a pitiful figure, but he reveals some strength of character, including a sense of humour. He is evidently at odds with both the archbishop and the chamberlain, who show him no respect. He bears the note of introduction written for Joan by de Baudricourt. The archbishop is intensely sceptical, and declares that Charles should not see the 'cracked country lass'. But the Dauphin is insistent that she is 'a saint: an angel' (p. 67). He is especially eager to receive her as visitations from saints have been a family tradition. La Hire interjects that the Maid, dressed as a soldier, is the angel that brought death to Foul Mouthed Frank. The archbishop assumes the voice of common sense, attributing the drowning to accident and the fulfilment of the prophecy to coincidence.

Discussion shifts to Joan's promise to lift the siege of Orleans, a feat that Jack Dunois has not yet managed to accomplish, despite his military reputation. It is eventually agreed that Joan should be admitted to the Court, and a simple test is planned; de Rais will pretend to be the Dauphin, and they will see whether Joan is fooled. The archbishop points out that common knowledge will enable her to make the distinction. Still, the test is staged in the main throne room. Bluebeard clearly relishes his role. Joan enters, dressed as a soldier, with bobbed hair. She sees through the pretence straight away, and in high spirits she draws the Dauphin from the assembled crowd, and announces her mission to see him crowned at Rheims.

The archbishop is moved by her faith, and declares that she is indeed sent by God. Accordingly, her wish to speak in private with the Dauphin should be respected. There ensues a dialogue between Joan and Charles, in which she tells him he must learn to behave like a king, and must fight the English. Riddled with self-doubt, he nonetheless pledges to fight and to become king. The court is summoned to return, and Charles announces that Joan now commands the army. La Trémouille reacts with hostility, but, supported by Joan, and through a great effort of will, the Dauphin dismisses him with a snap of his fingers. The knights of the Court rally to her and Joan falls to her knees to offer thanks to God. The others also kneel, as the archbishop gives a blessing. La Trémouille collapses, cursing.

> Essentially, this scene is an amplification of the first. Again we witness a sceptical response to reports of Joan's impact, but here the effect is intensified. There are three sceptics, rather than the single doubter of Scene I, and they are figures of greater social power. Her ability to convert reluctant men to her cause is emphatically portrayed here.
>
> In showing that the Lord Chamberlain has difficulty reading, George Bernard Shaw is indicating that literacy was rare at this time. He points out in the Preface that Joan was entirely illiterate, although she dictated letters, and held them to be of great importance.
>
> The Dauphin calls La Trémouille's threatening behaviour 'high treason' (p. 66). The terminology, which has more relevance to modern nations than to feudal Europe, would have been particularly meaningful to audiences at the end of the First World War, when treason was an emotive issue. For George Bernard Shaw, it had additional significance following recent trials in

Ireland. Joan is found guilty not of treason but, tried by an ecclesiastical court, of heresy.

Joan's accent and colloquial idiom contrast boldly with the speech of the Court. She cannot match the nobility in sophistication, but the intensity of her energy makes them appear dull. The test of her insight staged by de Rais is particularly unimaginative, and discloses an inclination to triviality and inconsequentiality. It is an important part of George Bernard Shaw's characterisation that Joan should not really be aware of the disruption she causes. Her actions have historical implications far beyond the limited scope of her comprehension.

The archbishop speaks of the dawning of a new age, which with the benefit of hindsight we can identify as the Renaissance. He accurately predicts that during this epoch the wisdom of pre-Christian thinkers, such as Aristotle and Pythagoras, will assume far greater importance than faith in saints and miracles. He comments that miracles are often, if not always, 'contrivances by which the priest fortifies the faith of his flock' (p. 71). Such a remark indicates that he is himself a transitional figure, his faith balanced by attachment to rationality in a manner that became the characteristic Renaissance orientation.

A scientific age will follow. But the reference to Pythagorean belief that the Earth is round and moves around the Sun raises an issue that George Bernard Shaw addressed in his Preface: respectable scientific theories, like long-respected religious beliefs, depend upon faith of a kind that may conflict with sensory evidence. Arguably, science has preserved blind faith amongst non-specialists, with scientists assuming the superior knowledge previously claimed by priests.

Joan may appear in her Christian zeal to be a figure belonging squarely to the earlier epoch, but her foreshadowing of Protestantism and nationalism arguably makes her more closely attuned to practical changes soon to occur in human social organisation than the archbishop is, despite his learning and his scepticism. But she is more single-minded in her religious faith than he is, and it is her ability to believe without a trace of scepticism that transforms her into a positive force.

SCENE III   **Joan meets the young general Jack Dunois on the bank of the river Loire, near Orleans. He is soon convinced that she is an appropriate leader for the army**

It is the evening of 29 April 1429, near the city of Orleans, which is besieged by the English. Dunois paces restlessly on the bank of the river Loire. He curses the west wind which hampers his efforts to lift the siege. His page draws attention to kingfishers flying across the river.

Dunois has eagerly awaited the arrival of the Maid, and when Joan appears, dressed in fine armour, he is too agitated to notice that the wind has dropped. Joan is annoyed that her troops have led her to the wrong side of the river for the intended challenge to the English. Dunois reveals that they were following his orders. He tries to give her a lesson in soldiering, but in response Joan simply asserts that she has come to do God's bidding. He remarks that she is in love with war, and she recalls the archbishop's insight that she is in love with religion.

Joan declares that she has no interest in romantic love or in money, supposedly the preoccupations of women. Instead, she is committed to soldiering. She advocates use of artillery, but Dunois still regards her as a religious figure, not as a soldier. Reaffirming her divinely ordained mission, she declares that the time for action has come. She agrees to go to church to pray for a change in the wind's direction, which will allow the river to be crossed on rafts. But the wind changes at once. Dunois takes this as a sign that Joan now commands the army. She embraces him, and they set off, ready for combat.

> Following the animated action of the last scene, George Bernard Shaw produces a marked change in dramatic effect. We now see Joan in conversation with Dunois, and their sense of fellowship is soon apparent. The brevity of the scene suggests a moment of relative calm between Joan's struggle to win approval and the battle that lies ahead.
>
> The sympathy between the two is readily comprehensible. Dunois is a man of action and a professional soldier, exemplifying the

courage and resourcefulness that Joan admires. He also has evident sensitivity, which fortifies the bond between them. As George Bernard Shaw makes clear in the Preface, historical evidence supports his own determination not to allow his heroine to be seen as a beautiful maiden from some romantic tale. Yet there does seem to be mutual attraction between the Maid and the military man in this scene. That impression is enhanced by the image of a pair of brilliant kingfishers, flying 'Like blue lightning' (p. 80). Still, references to love of war and love of religion suggest that the potentially amorous energy underlying the meeting is being directed on to another, impersonal plane. Joan does embrace Dunois, but as a comrade-in-arms. She also says, in matter-of-fact fashion, 'I will never take a husband', adding the historical detail: 'A man in Toul took an action against me for breach of promise; but I never promised him' (p. 83).

Is the change of the wind's direction following Joan's arrival a miracle, or mere coincidence? It is a question that tests modern audiences just as it tested Dunois. As the archbishop remarked in the previous scene, a miracle is whatever generates faith, and George Bernard Shaw required his audiences to have faith in the positive effects wrought by Joan's energies. She must also remain credible as a woman.

bend sinister in heraldry, a band on a family shield indicating illegitimacy

SCENE IV   **In a tent in the English camp, the Earl of Warwick and Bishop Cauchon discuss the significance of the Maid of Orleans. The earl identifies her Protestantism; the bishop speaks of her nationalism**

Inside a tent in the English camp, a chaplain (John de Stogumber) is writing, while a nobleman (Richard de Beauchamp, Earl of Warwick) peruses an illustrated book. The chaplain is concerned that the English have started to lose battles; Orleans went to the French, and a series of similar losses have followed. The nobleman replies, realistically, that only in books and ballads do enemies go always undefeated. The men regard Joan as sorceress. Warwick is more anxious about the proven capabilities of Dunois. Nonetheless, he plans to offer a large sum of money for the betrayal of Joan, who will then be burnt for witchcraft.

A page announces the arrival of the Bishop of Beauvais, Peter Cauchon. Warwick welcomes him warmly. They discuss the imminent coronation of Charles VII. It is agreed that the crowning of the Dauphin is a strategic master-stroke. The Englishmen advocate that Joan should be tried for sorcery, and burned if found guilty. De Stogumber is especially vehement. Cauchon is more measured in his evaluation, and insists that a French court should be involved. He points out that Joan carries the names of Christ and the Virgin Mary on her banner, and suggests that there might conceivably have been divine sanction for her actions, although he favours a theory that the devil has been involved. He is angered by Warwick's presumptuousness in assuming that he may act as the secular arm of the Church and oversee the burning of Joan. But the men are agreed that she poses a threat to them both and to the interests that they represent.

Warwick refers to Joan's Protestantism. Cauchon warns against the dangerous rise of nationalistic sentiment, which he regards as anti-Christian in its divisiveness since it amounts to the dethroning of Christ. De Stogumber argues the case for an 'England for the English' policy (p. 99). He claims that the English are a privileged people with 'peculiar fitness to rule over less civilized races for their own good' (p. 100).

> Following the conversational scene between Joan and Dunois, we now have a longer analysis of events between the Earl of Warwick, Chaplain de Stogumber and the Bishop of Beauvais. In this scene, the only one from which Joan is absent throughout, George Bernard Shaw makes explicit some of the major issues addressed in *Saint Joan*, notably the Maid's foreshadowing of Protestantism in religion, and nationalism in politics.

> Feudal fellowship allows the French bishop to enter the English camp and be warmly welcomed by the Earl of Warwick. The nobleman is keen to preserve the distinction between feudal territories such as Burgundy, Brittany, Picardy and Gascony, and deplores the notion of being classified as French or English: 'If this cant of serving their country once takes hold of them, goodbye to

the authority of their feudal lords, and goodbye to the authority of the Church' (p. 87).

Warwick is more willing to give credence to the power of Dunois, as a fellow Christian pilgrim to the Holy Land, than to that of a woman he prefers to regard as a 'village sorceress' (p. 87). The feudal system and the Catholic Church both had international orientation, fostering affinities that confirmed class and religious allegiances, to which national boundaries were considered irrelevant or inimical.

Warwick's family name is de Beauchamp, a clear reminder of the Norman dominance in English society since the conquest in 1066. This makes emphatic George Bernard Shaw's stress on the allegiance of the nobleman not to a nation, in the modern sense, but to a feudal class that was connected across territorial boundaries. When Cauchon refers to a French court, Warwick, wary of nationalist implications, is insistent on it being conceived as a Catholic court.

George Bernard Shaw holds names in reserve during the first part of the scene, foregrounding the men as types, in their opposition to Joan: nobleman and churchman. The introduction of proper names, all French in origin, cuts across the lines of demarcation anticipated by a modern audience, and shows just how radical Joan's incipient Protestant nationalism was. In that light, de Stogumber's crude patriotism appears decidedly **ironic**. He is especially vehement in his support for burning, and that intensity prepares us for the dramatic reversal he undergoes in Scene VI, after witnessing the execution. He is the opposite of Joan in that he seems entirely to lack imagination.

It is crucial to George Bernard Shaw's characterisation that the bishop is seen to be more measured and sensitive in his response to accusations of witchcraft. He insists on the processes of ecclesiastical law, and emphasises the need for fairness. Joan's victories can be explained in physical terms, and Cauchon is quick to acknowledge the role of Dunois in the recent successes. George Bernard Shaw was anxious that the bishop should not be seen as a fanatic, although he does read Joan's actions as diabolic in inspiration, and consequently he sees the threat she poses as levelled against the entire Catholic Church, and 'the souls of the entire human race' (p. 92).

When he speaks of the spread of heresy, Cauchon clearly has in mind the origins of what became Protestantism and created a vast rift within Christendom. His objection that Joan 'acts as if she herself were The Church' (p. 94) is exactly the charge that came to be levelled at later advocates of Protestant faith: 'It is always God and herself' (p. 95). The charge against her has to be heresy, rather than sorcery, and the bishop declares his first obligation to be salvation of the girl's soul.

Cauchon compares Joan to Mahomet, the camel driver who became a prophet and founded Islam, a faith that spread to the verges of medieval France. Both used letters to communicate God's will to political leaders. Joan's letters were necessarily dictated because she was illiterate, but the power of the written word began to grow in the late Middle Ages. A notably higher degree of general literacy helped give a distinctive character to the Renaissance which followed. George Bernard Shaw includes indications of this change as part of his portrayal of the processes of cultural evolution. So, at the start of the scene, Warwick extols the virtues of a well-made book, before adding, with a note of dismay: 'But nowadays, instead of looking at books, people read them' (p. 86). Importantly, during the Middle Ages reading and writing were largely the province of churchmen. The growth of Protestantism was accompanied by a need for every individual to be able to read the Bible. The spread of literacy was, then, a significant feature of the Protestant challenge to Roman Catholicism.

De Stogumber is outraged when Cauchon accuses Sir John Talbot of being 'a mad bull'. We learn that Talbot was 'three times Governor of Ireland' (p. 92). The installation of 'a mere fighting animal' (p. 90) in that powerful colonial position sums up, in George Bernard Shaw's view, the essential nature of English rule in Ireland. More generally, the presence of the English in France resonates with parallels of the British colonial presence in Ireland. In de Stogumber's dogmatic exclamation, 'How can what an Englishman believes be heresy? It is a contradiction in terms' (p. 96), George Bernard Shaw is signalling his own repugnance at latter-day English arrogance and insularity.

Cauchon refers to 'a Will to Power in the world' (p. 98). This 'Will' may be seen as the Life Force in which George Bernard Shaw placed his faith. The change it can effect is what Cauchon fears, and what George Bernard Shaw desired. The term 'Will to Power' was derived from the writings of Friedrich Nietzsche (1844–1900), a German philosopher on whose work George Bernard Shaw drew extensively in the formation of his own world-view. Feudal organisation was largely static, and involved minimal social change over a long period; the capitalist order that displaced it is characteristically dynamic.

Sir John Talbot 1st Earl of Shrewsbury (c.1384–1453), chief military commander during the final phase of the Hundred Years War

Mahomet George Bernard Shaw is reflecting the medieval Catholic response to Mahomet the prophet of Islam

Sancta simplicitas! a Latin phrase, literally sacred simplicity; it means something akin to 'ignorance is bliss'

SCENE V Following the coronation of Charles VII, Joan speaks with Dunois, the king, and the archbishop, within the cathedral at Rheims. It becomes apparent that despite her success she is an isolated and vulnerable figure

The setting is the cathedral at Rheims, immediately following the coronation of King Charles. Joan, dressed beautifully but still in masculine fashion, is praying. An organ is playing. As the music fades, Dunois appears, and tells Joan to desist praying as the people in the streets are calling for her. She has no desire to share the limelight with the king, and speaks of the fear she experiences before a battle, and boredom once the action has passed.

Dunois warns her that she has offended the powerful and the ambitious, and should expect them to seek revenge. She tells him, 'the world is too wicked for me' (p. 102). Only the saintly voices sustain her.

She hears them in the sound of church bells. Dunois considers her excessively fanciful.

The king appears, accompanied by Bluebeard and La Hire. Joan conceals herself behind a pillar. The king's remarks show him still to be a weak character; he has failed to take on the dignity of kingship along with its trappings. Joan emerges. She feels discouraged by Charles's inappropriate attitude and demeanour, and declares her intention to return to her father's farm. It is evident that she is not wanted at the Court, despite her role in crowning the Dauphin. He is clearly unsettled by her.

She then speaks, with apparent prescience, of her death. Dunois says that from recent experience he has learnt to take war seriously, and he is confident that he will drive the English from France. Joan wants to capture Paris before she departs, to ensure the king has his capital city. The prospect of further conflict horrifies the timid Charles.

The archbishop enters. He chastises Joan for not showing proper respect to the king and his Court. He accuses her of 'the sin of pride' (p. 106). Dunois advises that although she has had God on her side, and has consequently inspired her troops, she should not take for granted the continuance of God's support. He argues that the time has come for them to assume responsibility for their own work. He points to his own contribution as a general engaged in practical necessities, rather than a worker of miracles. But Joan counters that with the advent of gunpowder his conception of warfare is outmoded. She suggests that the men should be less obsessed with her perceived pride and more concerned with the truth she conveys.

Dunois cautions that Joan never counts the cost of her adventures, adding that 'she thinks she has God in her pocket' (p. 109). Her recklessness will lead to capture, with a prize of sixteen thousand pounds for her mercenary captor. When the mystique that surrounds her miracles is punctured, she will lose her following amongst the French troops. Charles says he will have no money to pay a ransom, and the archbishop announces, to her evident horror, that Joan, once captured, will be denounced as a witch.

Joan is forced to realise that she is effectively alone in the world of human affairs, but she sustains faith in her heavenly friends and advisers.

She concludes that 'the loneliness of God is His strength' (p. 112), and vows to draw strength from him until she meets her death. She departs, leaving the men impressed by her 'dangerous power', yet fearing the worst for her (p. 113).

Dunois calls Joan 'my little saint' (p. 101). It took until 1920 for the Church to endorse his estimation. George Bernard Shaw refers to the cathedral's bells as a medium for the voices Joan hears. His own view of her saintliness, as explained in the Preface, rejected supernatural influence, while affirming the intensity of her imagination. The sound of the bells acts as a focus for the vivid work of her imagination. When Charles asks why the voices do not visit him, as king, Joan replies: 'They do come to you; but you do not hear them' (p. 106). George Bernard Shaw believed that receptiveness was a quality crucial for greatness. Joan had the capacity to become an agent of the Life Force, enabling it to operate through her actions and words (see Theme on Creative Evolution and the Life Force).

To Dunois's observation, 'We never know when we are beaten', she retorts: 'You never know when you are victorious' (p. 106). The positive single-mindedness of her vision is a source of great strength, but it also results in a naive incapacity to grasp the political reality of her situation. She is incapable of understanding, until it is spelled out for her, that the men who wield power regard her as a threat, and will take drastic action to negate her influence.

Identifying Joan's pride, the archbishop remarks: 'The old Greek tragedy is rising among us. It is the chastisement of hubris' (p. 106). Despite her chirpy colloquial speech, Joan is intended as a tragic hero, and George Bernard Shaw makes that explicit here. 'Hubris' is the term used in Greek tragedy to identify self-confidence that blinds tragic figures to the inevitable fate that will follow their indifference to laws authorised by the gods. There are no gods of that order in George Bernard Shaw's play; rather, it is the nature of power, the character of those who possess it, and above all the weight of tradition, that determine the immediate outcome of Joan's life. It is the function of the play's Epilogue to show how

Joan, after her death, will rise above those factors that circumscribed her earthly fate.

Joan draws readily on proverbial wisdom, such as 'If ifs and ans were pots and pans there'd be no need of tinkers' (p. 108). This is the orally transmitted wisdom of a rural culture, using unsophisticated examples in readily remembered formulas. People of Joan's class inhabited a world without books, although before long literacy would cease to be the exclusive province of ecclesiastical scholars, and would fuel the Protestant spirit of the Reformation. Joan, despite her rustic manner, speaks for the future, not the past.

In particular, she understands that war has been altered by the invention of gunpowder. The impact of continuing technological change had been felt profoundly during the recent First World War. In his Preface George Bernard Shaw suggests that Joan's intuitive grasp of the nature of modern warfare foreshadowed the calculating strategies of Napoleon. In this scene, Bluebeard harks back to Caesar and Alexander for his sceptical comparisons. All were agents of significant historical change, but arguably Joan's example of Protestant nationalism has produced the most far-reaching legacy.

The archbishop attributes Joan's voices to her 'wilfulness' (p. 110). He is suggesting that she is obstinate, but the will to act has been a concern throughout the play. In the initial scene, de Baudricourt is seen to compensate for lack of will through bluster and bullying. The Dauphin's weakness is attributable to still greater deficiency of will. For George Bernard Shaw, the Will (or Life Force) was the motor of history, operating through certain individuals to effect change. Joan is, of course, just such an individual, and what the archbishop takes to be mere stubbornness is actually a manifestation of the Life Force finding an effective outlet (see Themes).

Joan has reached a crucial turning point in her life. Isolated, her fortunes now enter a downward spiral. She remarks here that she has always been alone, and refers to her father's threat to have her drowned if she failed to watch his sheep. George Bernard Shaw refers in the Preface to this blatant example of patriarchal

Scene v continued

oppression, an attempt to curb her attraction to soldiering, and to confine the young woman within the conventional limits allocated to her gender.

of Agincourt, of Poitiers and Crecy battles in the Hundred Years War

SCENE VI   **Joan's trial for heresy is staged at Rouen. She is found guilty and passed to the secular authorities for punishment. Chaplain de Stogumber, shocked by what he has witnessed, describes how she has been burnt at the stake**

A great hall in a castle at Rouen, on a fine sunny day, 30 May 1431, is the setting for the ecclesiastical trial. The Earl of Warwick enters, and is soon followed by Bishop Peter Cauchon, accompanied by Brother John Lemaître, a Dominican monk, and John D'Estivet, Canon of the Chapter of Bayeux. Warwick discusses with Cauchon the imminent trial of the Maid. The bishop explains that Lemaître, a representative of the Inquisition, is a specialist in combating heresy. D'Estivet will act as prosecutor of the case.

Warwick observes that it is nine months since Joan was taken prisoner by Burgundian troops. It is four months since he purchased her from their custody, before passing her to Cauchon as a suspected heretic. He is eager to have proceedings completed, and the Maid sentenced. The bishop explains that lengthy examination of the prisoner has been taking place.

Lemaître says he has detected grave heresy. This pleases Warwick, but Cauchon asserts his determination to ensure a fair trial for Joan, insisting that the Church must be just. The Inquisitor speaks of Cauchon's devotion to fair conduct, and of his determination to save the Maid's soul, if possible. Warwick's view is that Joan's death is 'a political necessity' (p. 117), but Cauchon angrily declares that the Church is not subject to such necessity. The Inquisitor states bluntly that Joan will die, because every utterance she makes convicts her.

Warwick departs, so the ecclesiastical court may assemble. Cauchon occupies one of the judicial seats, the Inquisitor takes the other. The assessors enter, led by de Stogumber and Canon de Courcelles. De Stogumber complains that the sixty-four-point indictment against Joan has been reduced without consultation. The Inquisitor replies that twelve charges will suffice. Cauchon agrees that heresy is the real issue, and speaks out against the arch-heresy of Protestantism, which poses a serious threat to the 'structure of Catholic Christendom' (p. 124).

Joan is admitted to the court, dressed in black and chained by the ankles. She shows physical signs that imprisonment has affected her adversely, but her vitality is still evident. She tells the bishop that a carp he sent for her meal has made her ill, and she complains that the English are unjust gaolers, determined to see her burnt as a witch. She asks why the Church does not oversee her captivity.

Martin Ladvenu, another Dominican monk, brings home to Joan the imminence of her execution through burning at a stake. She is horrified at the prospect, and looks around for help. Impetuously, she concedes that voices have devilishly led her to the verge of death. Ladvenu, believing that God has intervened to save her at the eleventh hour, hurriedly drafts a recantation, which he asks her to sign. She discloses that she cannot write her name, as she is illiterate.

De Stogumber is infuriated, sensing that the woman is slipping away from the doom he desires for her. He declares that the English will kill her anyway, and calls Cauchon a traitor. Still, Ladvenu reads the recantation to Joan. She signs, assisted by Ladvenu's guiding hand, but as a stage direction indicates, she is *tormented by the rebellion of the soul against her mind and body* (p. 136). The Inquisitor declares her free from the threat of excommunication, and Joan thanks him. He then announces that on account of her sins she is condemned to spend the rest of her days 'in perpetual imprisonment' (p. 137). Joan is shocked, and, tearing up the signed document, she affirms that her voices were right, and demands that the fire be prepared for her burning. She confronts her accusers with the charge that they follow the devil, while she follows God.

The executioner and his assistants leave to prepare the flames. Joan declares that it is God's will that she should 'go through the fire to His bosom' (p. 138). Cauchon and the Inquisitor pronounce her excommunication, and pass her over to the secular powers, with an admonition to them to show compassion in the mode of execution. Joan is led from the court. The assessors depart, with the exception of Ladvenu, who is appalled at the outcome. The judges ask him to oversee the proper conduct of the execution, but he intends to stand at Joan's side as sympathiser rather than persecutor.

Cauchon deplores the manner in which the English are staging the burning. The Inquisitor is more reconciled to the course of events and declares: 'One gets used to it. Habit is everything. I am accustomed to the fire: it is soon over' (p. 139). Unexpectedly, he argues that Joan is innocent, in the sense that her ignorance was her downfall.

Warwick enters. The Inquisitor leaves to witness the end of the execution. It is clear that Warwick and Cauchon have disparate views as regards the extent of their authority. The bishop departs. After a short while, Warwick is joined by de Stogumber. He was the most vociferous advocate of burning for the witch, but now he is tormented by what he has witnessed. In the midst of the horror, Joan called out to Christ. She asked for a cross, and was given one, hastily contrived from two sticks. De Stogumber is horrified that some people laughed at her, and he suggests they would have made fun of Christ at His crucifixion.

Ladvenu arrives, carrying a bishop's cross. He asserts that Joan's death showed her to be blessed by Christ, and suggests that her physical death was merely the beginning of a new mode of existence. De Stogumber rushes wildly from the room declaring himself a Judas, who should take his own life. Warwick sends Ladvenu to constrain the chaplain. As he exits, the Master Executioner of Rouen appears, and announces proudly that Warwick's bidding has been done. Joan's remains have been disposed of in the river, although her heart would not burn. When he tells Warwick that he has heard the last of her, the earl smiles uneasily, recalling Ladvenu's words to the contrary.

> This is not trial by jury under civil law, but is an ecclesiastical court, addressing heresy. De Stogumber and Courcelles press for criminal charges to be levelled, but the judges refuse to allow such trivialities to occupy the time of their court. George Bernard Shaw sets out to restore the reputation of Joan's judges, which has been subject to defamation following her posthumous rehabilitation. It is important to his purpose that the bishop and the Inquisitor are seen to be acting in good faith; Joan is challenging the fundamentals of their world-view, and their reaction should not be seen as shallow malice. George Bernard Shaw wants us to recognise that this is an

extremely significant historical moment, so we must not be distracted by suspicion that this is a petty clash of personalities, or a mere divergence of opinions. Thus, the Inquisitor speaks out against cruelty, and Cauchon condemns torture and 'forced confessions' (p. 127).

Crucially, Joan refuses to deny that the voices she heard came directly from God. In privileging her own judgement above that of the Church she condemns herself. Ladvenu identifies in her 'a terrible pride and self-sufficiency' (p. 132). Roman Catholicism insists on the need for priests, and the mediation of the institution between individual worshippers and their God. It was one of the principal innovations of Protestantism to argue against the need for such mediation, and to stress the importance of the individual's direct relationship with God.

In medieval Europe, church services were invariably conducted in Latin, a language ordinary members of the congregation did not understand, while the ability to read the scriptures was the province of priests and monks alone. Protestantism required individual church members to be able to read the Bible, so the spread of literacy and use of vernacular languages was encouraged. In this scene, we are again reminded that Joan is illiterate and needs assistance even to write her name. Her spirit might have been Protestant, but the times were Roman Catholic, and that tension lies at the heart of her tragedy.

Reference is made to Joan's attempt to escape by leaping from a tower sixty feet high. Such an act would appear tenable only for someone with supernatural powers, and it is significant that although she dared to make the jump, Joan was injured in the process. This future saint was not blessed with capabilities denied to other human beings; rather, George Bernard Shaw insists, she was reckless in her single-mindedness. Her recklessness might be perceived as foolishness, but it is a manifestation of that same strength of will which enabled her to inspire those soldiers who followed her. She was not different in kind, but manifested greater intensity of purpose than most other people.

Warwick's allegiance to the order upheld by the feudal aristocracy takes precedence over his observance of religious imperatives, to the point of risking damnation, in the bishop's view. Feudalism and the medieval Catholic Church were based on assumptions that were essentially international. At this point in history, it was becoming evident that despite their shared horizons there was no guarantee of an alignment of interests between the institutions. Indeed, the Inquisitor declares that 'All secular power makes men scoundrels' (p. 118). There are clear indications that the old European social and cultural order is starting to disintegrate.

Through his characterisation of de Stogumber, George Bernard Shaw, the Irish dramatist, continues his attack on English arrogance. The chaplain believes that the voices of saints heard by Joan would necessarily have spoken English. George Bernard Shaw detected an assumption amongst the English of divinely ordained privilege. But note that Joan takes a common language to be the basis for shared national identity. **Ironically,** a solid grounding for nationalist sentiment, so greatly feared by the feudal order, is already evident in de Stogumber's chauvinism. His name is French, but his outlook is aggressively English, with all the insularity that this might imply from a continental European point of view. The chaplain is Joan's most vociferous opponent, but his crude sense of national identity makes him in effect her close ally. Perhaps the shock he experiences when witnessing her burning at the end of the scene is not such a complete reversal as it initially appears.

The Inquisitor notes that heresies often begin with saintly simplicity. This is an important observation, for George Bernard Shaw recognised that a very thin line separated heresy and saintliness in a case such as Joan's. If the Church accepted the authenticity of her voices and visions then she would be a saint; if it denied their divine origin, she would be a heretic. This is the pivotal point on which the historical reversal of Joan's reputation rested.

The Inquisitor is allowed a long **soliloquy** in which he condemns the dangers of unorthodox behaviour. This outlook will offend modern liberal sensibilities, but George Bernard Shaw has Lemaître speak emphatically against cruelty. This may seem to contradict the popular view of the Inquisition, as an institution that operated with uncompromising severity, but George Bernard Shaw's point is that secular morality is inadequate to grasp the compassionate basis of Inquisitorial judgement, summed up in the declaration that 'if you hate cruelty, remember that nothing is so cruel in its consequences as the toleration of heresy' (p. 123). Within the terms of his understanding of the world, Lemaître is a man of real integrity, although we should not overlook his declaration that habit has inured him to public burnings. When a meaningful system for living is reduced to the dull workings of habit, some form of change is surely necessary.

Joan confronts her inquisitors with an earthy common sense. There is a clear disjunction between their sophisticated understanding and her own impassioned but simple beliefs. Employing characteristically colloquial idiom she calls her prosecutor, Courcelles, 'a rare noodle' because he mindlessly follows precedent (p. 128). The effect is comic, especially when Courcelles repeats the term. George Bernard Shaw seeks to intensify the audience's feeling of warmth towards the artless honesty of the Maid. But it is important to recognise that precedent was paramount in this feudal, Catholic society, with its resistance to change and its respect for established authority. Joan's rejection of the patterns of the past was nothing short of revolutionary.

The characterisation of Cauchon becomes a matter of great importance at this stage of the play. He has the perspicacity to see how Joan's Protestant denials of the Church threaten its future, and he responds with a sense of the historical moment, rather than reacting with the hostility of blind prejudice. He laments the barbarity of the English soldiers who conduct the burning. Cauchon is keen to halt their impropriety. The Inquisitor advises him not to hurry; the court itself has proceeded correctly, and if the English now violate the proper order of execution it 'may be useful later on: one never knows' (p. 139). This prescient insight suggests that Lemaître would not have been entirely surprised that, five hundred years later, Joan would be canonised as a saint by that very Church that had excommunicated her, and had handed her over to her doom. He recognises the quality of innocence within the guileless young woman.

Warwick remarks to Ladvenu that Joan's case is concluded. The monk replies enigmatically that 'It may have just begun' (p. 142). Here is further apparent prescience, with another intelligent and sensitive member of the Catholic Church recognising some of the implications for history of Joan's life and death. The comment also serves to prepare the audience for the surprises in the Epilogue.

the Holy Office the Inquisition

Moab region of Jordan, to the east of the Dead Sea

Ammon region to the north of Moab

St Athanasius (*c*.296–AD373) Bishop of Alexandria for forty-five years, commencing in AD328

EPILOGUE   **On a stormy night, twenty-five years after the execution, Martin Ladvenu enters the king's bedchamber to announce that Joan has been rehabilitated. After his departure, Joan appears before the king, followed by Cauchon, Dunois, an English soldier, de Stogumber, the executioner and Warwick. A modern clergyman arrives with news that Joan has been made a saint. The archbishop and the Inquisitor enter, and all pay homage to her. Then, the king returns to his bed, the other men depart, and Joan is left alone to deliver the play's final words**

It is June 1456, twenty-five years after Joan's execution. A period of hot weather has culminated in a stormy night. The former Dauphin, now King Charles VII of France, is fifty-one years old, and is known as Charles the Victorious. In his bedchamber, the king reclines, looking at a book. He whirls a rattle, and Martin Ladvenu enters the chamber. Charles, who does not know Ladvenu, leaps from his bed, disturbed and fearful.

Ladvenu announces solemnly that the taint has been removed from the king. He refers to an inquiry, just completed, which has reviewed Joan's case. Although this procedure has overturned the authority of the initial judgement, and has exonerated Joan, the monk is adamant that the original trial was properly conducted, and was merciful. But the secular punishment, the burning, was wrong, and now, he says, 'the true heart that lived through the flame is consecrated' (p. 145).

The king is relieved to hear that the charge that he was crowned by a witch and a heretic will no longer be levelled. Joan has been rehabilitated, and the sentence passed on her has been annulled. Ladvenu is more concerned with the implications for Joan, but the king insists that if she were to return she would soon be burned again, despite the current adoration. She was one of a kind, and they should not concern themselves with her. Ladvenu is incensed and departs, vowing to stay clear of kings in future.

Left alone, Charles wonders where his servants are. Then, amid strong wind and summer lightning, the figure of Joan appears, declaring herself a figment in a dream. Charles admits he has drawn courage from Joan's own bravery. He also derived strength from the example of his former mistress, Agnes Sorel, now dead.

He says that following Joan's execution her mother and brothers called for a retrial, and now she has been officially declared a victim of corrupt judges. But Joan defends her judges. The figure of Peter Cauchon appears, relating how his corpse was excommunicated, exhumed and cast into a common sewer.

The ghostly figure of Dunois emerges and confirms that the English have been driven from France. He is still alive, but his spirit has entered this dreamy scene. After a while, a rough English soldier joins them, singing coarsely. This is the soldier who gave Joan two sticks to form a crucifix, as she burned. He is allowed one day a year remission from hell. He announces that hell is a 'treat' after fifteen years serving in the French wars, and reveals that it is filled with eminent men.

De Stogumber, formerly the aggressive chaplain, enters. He has gone a little mad since witnessing the death of Joan, and is now a benign old village parson. The executioner follows, and says that de Stogumber is less alive than Joan, whose heart would not burn. Warwick appears and congratulates Joan on her rehabilitation. Duplicitously, he apologises with an assurance that the burning was political necessity rather than personal malice. Joan harbours no resentment. The earl foresees the day when she will be made a saint.

A clergyman appears, dressed in the fashion of 1920, which the others regard as comic dress. He responds with dry formality, announcing the canonisation of Saint Joan. A vision of her statue in Winchester Cathedral is seen momentarily. Another, from Rheims Cathedral, then appears. Dunois calls her 'the soul of France' (p. 157).

The archbishop and the Inquisitor appear, standing on either side of Cauchon. The men on stage kneel before Saint Joan in an act of devotion. All are alarmed, however, when Joan raises the prospect of her return as a living woman. They depart, one by one. Charles returns to bed, and Joan wishes him goodnight.

The soldier remains to condemn the treachery of kings, captains, bishops and lawyers. He is about to deliver a lecture when the clock strikes midnight and he has to return to hell. A white radiance surrounds Joan as she delivers the play's plaintive final words: 'O God that madest this beautiful earth, when will it be ready to receive Thy saints? How long, O Lord, how long?' (p. 159).

This concluding scene of the play . has generated controversy amongst critics and reviewers. In place of the persuasive realism of the earlier scenes, we are confronted with a fantastic dream sequence.

Ladvenu expresses disapproval of the way in which Joan's judges have been reviled, even as he welcomes her rehabilitation. George Bernard Shaw continues to emphasise that in excommunicating Joan the judges were acting in accordance with their deeply held beliefs. It was secular power that perpetrated the burning, indulging a coarse appetite for violence and revenge. There is a clash of divergent world-views at the heart of this case, and George Bernard Shaw is keen to preclude it being perceived as crude prejudice on the part of the judiciary.

The apparition of Peter Cauchon, who has suffered posthumous ignominy, underlines the fact that he was driven by a genuine and enduring sense of justice. It is the changing world that has lost sight of this particular conception of justice. Joan actually says that she wants men to benefit from remembering her, and remarks that she would be far less well remembered if Cauchon had not pronounced her a heretic. The bewildered Cauchon asks: 'Must then a Christ perish in torment in every age to save those that have no imagination?' (p. 154). Parallels between Joan's execution and the crucifixion of Jesus are implied at regular intervals in the play; here the identification is at its most explicit.

Charles takes pride in leaving the world as it is; he criticises Joan's desire to transform and effect change. This is a measure of his debilitating lack of will. George Bernard Shaw felt strongly that the rulers of the earth were rarely the figures who added fuel to the real motor of history. As if to elucidate that point, the modern concept of nationalism is brought to the fore once more, with discussion of the rout of the English. Dunois has survived his soldiering, and part of the credit for this must go to the lessons he has learnt from Joan. She may be seen to have initiated a new seriousness in the conduct of warfare, as was appropriate to the modern sense of nationhood.

Joan's brand of individualism involved a freedom of spirit that could not face the life of perpetual imprisonment offered by the Inquisition as an alternative to death by burning. The free spirit could not be tolerated in such a rigidly codified culture, and although Saint Joan comes to be revered, the prospect of her physical return horrifies the other characters. Their cowering departure indicates George Bernard Shaw's sense that an agent of the Life Force will always cause unease, even terror, during her or his lifetime. As George Bernard Shaw signals through the boldly **anachronistic** inclusion of a modern clergyman, critical hindsight is required to comprehend the crucial impact of such a life. Human societies invariably fear the turbulence of such a transforming presence.

Fouquet's Boccaccio Jean Fouquet (*c*.1420–*c*.1480), French illustrator of books including an edition of the *Decameron* by the Italian author Giovanni Boccaccio (1313–75)

Charlemagne Charles I of France (*c*.742–814), known as Charles the Great, who conquered nearly all of the Christian countries of Europe, thereby unifying them as a single empire

King David (d. *c*.962BC) second king of the Israelites, who established Israel as a united kingdom, with Jerusalem as its capital. In Jewish tradition, the ideal ruler

CRITICAL APPROACHES

CHARACTERISATION

At a time when renewed interest in psychology had been stimulated by the innovative interpretations offered by Sigmund Freud (1856–1939), with his psychoanalytic theory, George Bernard Shaw's emphasis falls on action and event rather than upon interior states. In his Preface, he draws upon recent psychological studies to produce modern interpretations of Joan's proclivity to visionary experiences, but on stage there is no introspective analysis of this kind.

JOAN

The stage directions accompanying her initial entry in Scene I identify Joan as a country girl in her late teens. Although she is a young woman from the middle ranks of society, she has to carry an enormous weight of significance in George Bernard Shaw's play. Not only is she a soldier destined for sainthood, she is also the prototype nationalist and Protestant, foreshadowing the future history of Europe.

Yet her appearance is ordinary, although she does have '*eyes very wide apart and bulging as they often do in very imaginative people*' (p. 52). George Bernard Shaw makes clear in his Preface that he needed to show her as a character unexceptional except in the intensity of her imagination and the strength of her will. It is her energy and capacity for action that differentiate Joan from those around her.

George Bernard Shaw's Joan is stripped of mystique; she is a simple young woman, who speaks plainly and acts decisively. Her effectiveness stems from that decisiveness: determined not to be carried along by events, she renounces passivity, and devotes her energies to shaping what happens. Yet she is not self-conscious, even though she alters the course of history. Driven by faith, she rises to the challenge posed by all obstacles, and gets things done.

In his Preface, George Bernard Shaw sums up Joan as 'the sort of woman that wants to lead a man's life' (p. 20). George Bernard Shaw felt that the familiar historical portrayals of Joan had contrived to avoid acknowledging that this young woman had succeeded through the exercise of abilities usually considered to be exclusively masculine. He regarded such characterisation as 'Anti-Feminist' (see Contemporary Approaches – Feminist Criticism). In fact, he felt that men and women were fundamentally the same, and critics have frequently remarked that his own Joan is an androgynous figure; that is, she combines attributes conventionally associated with both masculinity and femininity.

A prominent aspect of her characterisation is her insistence on wearing soldiers' apparel, conventionally masculine dress. She is at first dressed 'respectably', with no hint of impropriety, but in red, a colour with associations of passion and vitality. Her subsequent refusal to adopt recognised trappings of femininity is a major point of contention in the play. Male figures of authority insist that Joan should conform to the subordinate role assigned to her within society, but she refuses. Her soldierly costume is a constant reminder of her rebelliousness, and of her practicality. She is as capable as any man of leading an army in battle, but women's dress would inevitably hinder her activity, physically. It would also, by highlighting her gender, preclude her from assuming a commanding role in a male-dominated society.

If clothing sends a signal to the eyes of members of the audience, their ears receive comparable clues from Joan's accent and idiom. She speaks a homely form of northern English, and her colloquial style is peppered with down-to-earth images. It is a direct and practical mode of speaking, without pretension and free from displays of conventional reverence towards her supposed social superiors.

Homely she may sound, but Joan rejects the Inquisitor's description of her as 'a shepherd lass' (p. 128). She insists that at home she does the work of the lady of the house, spinning and weaving. George Bernard Shaw's Preface supports the view that she was a member of the middle, rather than the lower classes. The same broad social category formed the bulk of George Bernard Shaw's first audiences. So, although social relationships had assumed a markedly different character in the intervening centuries, there were grounds for a bridge of sympathy between the onlookers in the auditorium and the heroine on stage. The audience's identification with her social status had the additional value of supporting George Bernard Shaw's argument that she was essentially an ordinary person, and certainly not a freak.

Still, Joan is a rebel, rejecting gender stereotypes and ignoring conventional expectations. She wears her hair short and dresses as a man. Audiences would have recognised that as a form of feminist provocation, familiar enough in the early decades of the twentieth century. George Bernard Shaw saw the daughters of middle-class families as invaluable converts to his cause of shedding the dead weight of tradition, with its inbuilt injustice and delimiting assumptions.

Joan's characteristic self-assurance and assertiveness follow from her profound yet lively faith. The archbishop remarks that she is 'in love with religion' (p. 73). Although Joan is a member of an orthodox Roman Catholic society, she believes that she can bypass the institution of the Church, and establish a direct relationship with God. In this respect she heralds the advent of Protestant Christianity, with its rejection of the authority of priests and its stress upon individual conscience. In the play, the Earl of Warwick identifies her faith as 'Protestantism' (p. 99). In a letter written in 1922 to his friend Father Joseph Leonard, George Bernard Shaw described Joan as 'the first Protestant saint and martyr'. Indeed, he considered her the first nationalist and the first Protestant, foreshadowing the future history of western European civilisation.

George Bernard Shaw's Joan is a robust character with a pronounced sense of humour. Her informality, often bordering on cheekiness, is designed to appeal to modern democratic taste, and her vitality is contrary to the familiar conception of saintliness as an ascetic and unworldly state. She is pious, but also a character who laughs and cries. Her main flaw, the immediate cause of her death, is an innocence that prevents her recognising the animosity aroused in others by the overwhelming self-confidence of her declarations and her actions. But in the long term, that innocence may be seen as a necessary ingredient of her ultimate success, enabling her to act, in George Bernard Shaw's terms, as an effective agent of the Life Force (see Theme on Creative Evolution and the Life Force).

The Italian playwright Luigi Pirandello argued that Joan was a reflection of George Bernard Shaw's sense of his own historical significance. Support for this view might be drawn from the fact that

George Bernard Shaw had a statue of the saint placed in the garden of his home at Ayot St Lawrence, in Hertfordshire.

CAPTAIN ROBERT DE BAUDRICOURT

De Baudricourt is the first character we meet in the play. He is a handsome and physically energetic military squire, with all the appearance of a effective man of action. But, crucially, he lacks will-power, and squanders his potential to act through launching temperamental and unproductive verbal assaults on his steward. His ineffectualness, despite the promise of his outward appearance, contrasts dramatically with Joan's single-minded drive, combined with her outward inappropriateness, in conventional terms, as a military leader.

BERTRAND DE POULENGEY

In his mid thirties, 'Polly', as Joan insists on calling him, is described in the stage directions as *'dreamily absent-minded, seldom speaking unless spoken to, and then slow and obstinate in reply'* (p. 55). The contrast to the focused and voluble Joan is obvious.

GILLES DE RAIS

Despite a show of agreeableness, de Rais is capable of extreme cruelty, as historical record testifies. In fact, his popular name, 'Bluebeard' has become synonymous with savage brutality. George Bernard Shaw could rely upon members of his audience knowing this, and he notes in his stage directions that de Rais was executed some years later, on account of his barbarous acts. Yet de Rais declares himself the archbishop's 'faithful lamb' (p. 64). The pungent **irony** of this declaration highlights the man's duplicity, which contrasts with Joan's simple directness and honesty.

THE DAUPHIN

The man who, with Joan's help, becomes King Charles VII is handicapped by timidity. Tradition dictates that he should take the throne, but as soon as he appears on stage it is evident that he is not naturally equipped to be a ruler. He is aware of this, and is nervous of assuming responsibility. George Bernard Shaw is keen to make the point that those in power are often not those best suited to govern in the interests of all. But the Dauphin's self-awareness, at least, is to his credit, and although weak he is by no means a fool.

The contrast between Joan's boldness and his diffidence is very striking, and leads to some comic moments. It also illustrates George Bernard Shaw's contention that conventionally masculine attributes are not to be found in all men, any more than they are excluded from all women.

Charles's situation draws attention to the power of the aristocracy in this feudal society. He owes money to his lords, and they regard him with contempt. He also shows himself ungrateful, failing to offer thanks to Joan following his coronation. But he is a survivor, and as we learn from the Epilogue, once Joan has helped make him king he rules effectively, despite the shortcomings of his character. In that final scene he attributes his eventual successes to Joan's example, and to the support he received from another woman, Agnes Sorel.

EARL OF WARWICK

Richard de Beauchamp, the Earl of Warwick, is the commander of the English army in France. Worldly and alert to political realities, he gives voice to the anxieties of his class, the feudal aristocracy, at a time when it seems to face imminent crisis. His dedication to his class takes precedence over religious considerations, and he fears the rise of nationalism. In calling for enhanced power for the king, Joan declares herself his enemy, challenging the feudal principles he holds most dear. Her destruction becomes an imperative for him as the play unfolds, and he calls for her execution. He is ruthless and resourceful, but historically his day has passed, and he seems to intuit Joan's long-term victory. The expedient nature of his actions indicates the decay of those ideals which had formed a strong centre, holding feudal society together for centuries.

PETER CAUCHON, BISHOP OF BEAUVAIS

George Bernard Shaw took pains to create an understanding that Cauchon was a fair man who acted scrupulously in his conduct of Joan's trial. His serious observance of religious law is evident in his focused concern with Joan's alleged heresy. He loses his temper when the prosecutors revert obtusely to trivial issues, such as whether Joan stole a horse. Importantly, he is presented not as a prejudiced man keen for vengeance, but as a steadfast member of the Church, who feels a burden of genuine responsibility for the salvation of Joan's soul. He pronounces her excommunication with solemn gravity, and is horrified by the improper haste of her execution.

In the Epilogue his ghost appears and laments the vilification he endured following Joan's rehabilitation. He is aggrieved at the treatment he received, but is still more concerned that this sequence of events foreshadows dramatic and, to him, disastrous changes in the constitution of the Christian world.

THE INQUISITOR

Brother John Lemâitre is a pious member of the Church, who conducts his duties with disciplined professionalism. He is really the controlling figure at the trial, clear-sighted and subtle in his dealings with others. An expert in Church law, he is committed to countering heresy, which he sees as the work of the devil, yet he is sensitive to accusations that the Inquisition is a cruel institution. As he says:

> though the work I have to do may seem cruel to those who do not know how much more cruel it would be to leave it undone, I would go to the stake myself sooner than do it if I did not know its righteousness, its necessity, its essential mercy. (p. 123)

He is a highly articulate and persuasive orator. He regards Joan with greater detachment than Cauchon does, but is equally concerned for the fate of her soul.

THE ARCHBISHOP

The Archbishop of Rheims dismisses claims that Joan has performed miracles, and advises that she should not be admitted to the Dauphin's

Court. He is shrewd enough to recognise, however, that she is an inspirational figure, who may serve Charles's cause. He also recognises her genuine piety, and remarks that Joan is in love with religion. His own approach to religious observance has a rather more practical orientation, and he suspects that her zeal will lead her into serious trouble. The archbishop is a dignified churchman, but his evident rationality compromises his faith, indicating that he is ultimately more attuned to the enquiring spirit of the future than the dogmatic beliefs of the past.

MARTIN LADVENU

Martin Ladvenu is a Dominican monk, a compassionate and considerate figure, who sincerely cares for Joan. He makes a case for simplicity, a form of innocence, being the cause of Joan's lapse into heresy, rather than the intervention of the devil that the Inquisitor suspects. Nonetheless, Ladvenu supports the objectives of the Inquisition. He is instrumental in securing the recantation that looks set to save her life, and is shocked when she again lapses into heresy. He regards her burning with composed solemnity, but in the Epilogue he demonstrates continued support for her, as an advocate for her rehabilitation. Taken in conjunction with Lemâitre, Ladvenu shows that George Bernard Shaw did not wish the Inquisition to be seen as a sadistic aberration, but as a well-intentioned component of the Church, the integrity of which it sought to preserve.

JOHN DE STOGUMBER

The bigoted and crude English chaplain initially appears to be a comic character. He provides a vehicle by means of which George Bernard Shaw **satirises** the opinionated arrogance of English chauvinism. His religious belief is dogmatic and unthinking. He declares with characteristic bluntness: 'Certainly England for the English goes without saying: it is the simple law of nature' (p. 99). This nationalism is inconsistent with the feudal world, and signals insular English readiness to put up national barriers, conceiving all foreigners as inferior. Perhaps George Bernard Shaw was drawing upon the worst excesses of patriotic fervour witnessed during the recent war. But as an Irishman George Bernard Shaw would have been especially sensitive to de Stogumber's allusion to England's 'legitimate conquests, given her by God because of her peculiar fitness to rule over less civilized races for their own good' (p. 100).

His boorishness has an important dramatic function because, for all his apparent callousness, the chaplain is affected profoundly by Joan's burning. In stark contrast to the Maid, de Stogumber lacks imagination; he needs to witness suffering before it can acquire meaning for him. His reaction is quite unexpected, a striking reversal in which he is overwhelmed by guilt and a sense of pity. George Bernard Shaw uses him to show how basic attitudes can be reversed through experience of physical realities. In the Epilogue, he appears as a gentle, rather feeble old man, still bound by his limitations, and incapable himself of becoming an agent for human advancement, yet affected significantly by Joan's presence in his life.

DUNOIS, THE BASTARD OF ORLEANS

This young general, the illegitimate son of Louis, Duc d'Orléans, is the only character, apart from Ladvenu, to extend real friendship to Joan. Jack Dunois is shown to be of a poetic and sensitive, yet courageous temperament. He has the attributes of a standard **romantic** hero, handsome and daring. But George Bernard Shaw was a realist, and rejected the delusions engendered by romantic fictions. So the chivalric Dunois is effectively consigned to the past, as Joan instructs him in the proper conduct of modern warfare. His approach to combat retains rituals that render it an elaborate game. Her approach is hard-headed, practical and relentlessly realistic. He has to change in order to survive as an effective soldier.

Their meeting in Scene III contains ingredients of a conventional love scene; for example, Dunois watches a pair of kingfishers fly across the river, and the birds suggest a possible parallel to him and Joan. But as George Bernard Shaw has made clear in his Preface, Joan subordinates feelings of love, or sexual attraction, to the requirements of effective soldiering. George Bernard Shaw considered sex a distraction from serious issues.

At the time this play was written, a significant number of novelists and poets, including James Joyce, Gertrude Stein, T.S. Eliot and Ezra Pound, were producing work that posed a challenge to their readers, presenting them with obscure words or unfamiliar sentence structures, and a dense or fragmented style. Such difficult work initially found a relatively small readership, and demanded the investment of considerable time and effort from individual readers. George Bernard Shaw's primary concern, however, was to communicate directly and effectively with a group; his aim was to fortify or modify attitudes and views held by his audiences. Consequently, *Saint Joan* was written with plain directness, posing no problems to intelligibility.

George Bernard Shaw was renowned for his ability to write witty dialogue, but there is no effort to dazzle with style in this play. The challenge posed by making a medieval subject appear realistic and relevant doubtless persuaded him to avoid the potential distractions of embellishment. The dialogue has a liveliness derived from variety, however, with Joan speaking a stylised form of colloquial northern English, in contrast to the more formal language and idiom used by the socially elevated characters.

Other characters, such as La Hire and de Stogumber, speak more coarsely, the former in the manner of a soldier, the latter as a boorish Englishman. The Dauphin, whose character does not match his inherited status, speaks with tell-tale informality. His conversational manner is designed to make him, to some extent, a likeable character, despite his flaws. Simultaneously, it discloses a lack of those serious qualities that distinguish able political leaders.

Bishop Cauchon is an elegant speaker, but George Bernard Shaw avoids the sense that his finesse is superficial. His propensity to employ boldly figurative speech and to make impressive general statements is indicative of passionate commitment to the faith that underpins his urbane social manner. The Inquisitor speaks with more detachment, keeping his observations measured and prudent, although he is equally committed in his beliefs. He has the rhetorical skill of the lawyer, a talent for persuasion. Despite their differing styles of utterance both men share a genuine concern for Joan's salvation, and in their distinctive ways both convey that seriousness.

In contrast to the formal language of the Dauphin's Court and of the ecclesiastical trial, Joan's pithy conciseness suggests honest simplicity and a down-to-earth nature. George Bernard Shaw is defusing any suggestion that the visionary Maid is ethereal or unworldly, although she is capable of lyricism when referring to the voices she hears. Her regional accent grounds her in a locality, her speech reflecting the character of the place where she has grown up. This is appropriate thematically, as Joan advocates recognition of distinctive national identity, grounded in place and common language, as a corrective to the international identity assumed by the aristocracy and churchmen. Her vocabulary and syntax display local idiosyncrasies, but these are never so marked as to hinder comprehension.

For an extended discussion of George Bernard Shaw's language in *Saint Joan*, see John A. Mills, *Language and Laughter: Comic Diction in the Plays of Bernard Shaw* (University of Arizona Press, Tucson, 1969).

DRAMATIC TECHNIQUE & STRUCTURE

In terms of action, the structure of *Saint Joan* is straightforward; the play's complexity arises on the level of the ideas that inform it. George Bernard Shaw condensed his treatment of Joan into six scenes. The first three follow her rise from obscurity to historical significance, with the siege of Orleans providing the focal point. The concluding three chart her loss of influence and her death. Scene VI presents the trial which is in many ways the dramatic focus as well as the climax of the story. It is in effect a play within the play, requiring the appearance of certain characters who have a key role to enact, but who have not appeared previously. The Epilogue entails two historical leaps forward, to the rehabilitation trial of 1456, and the canonisation that occurred in 1920.

In Scenes III and IV, George Bernard Shaw boldly locates conversation at that point where the most intense dramatic action might be anticipated. Between these two central scenes, the critical shift in Joan's fortunes from ascendancy to decline occurs. She is absent from the stage for roughly half of the play. Only in the fifth scene is she present throughout. But importantly, she is entirely absent from Scene IV. The siege has been raised, the coronation has yet to occur. Yet even in her absence Joan is the focus for discussion amongst the other characters. In this way George Bernard Shaw delineates the impact she is having, not just in direct material terms, but as an agent of profound social and cultural change. Politics, religion and economics are all modified by her actions in ways that might not be immediately apparent. As Cauchon and Warwick make their evaluation, the large-scale implications become clearer.

George Bernard Shaw, unlike Shakespeare in comparable situations, and unlike his own practice in *Caesar and Cleopatra*, here forgoes the opportunity to stage battle scenes, despite Joan's martial prowess. Shakespeare, in *Henry VI, Part I*, made Joan very much a warrior figure, and George Bernard Shaw's approach shows his concern to create a very different figure. More importantly, isolating her from the collective action of battle places great weight on the value of her own individual life and death. Especially in the wake of the recent war, George Bernard Shaw was keen to prevent any glamour accruing to warfare, and the mass slaughter of that conflict had effectively diminished the significance of an individual human life in a way that goes against the grain of George Bernard Shaw's portrayal.

The Epilogue has been a major point of critical concern since the first performance. Is it an essential and integrated component of the drama? Or is it a superfluous addition, positioned uneasily after the play has effectively finished? It is a long scene, and markedly different in tone from what has preceded it. Reviewers such as James Agate and A.N. Kaul declared it unnecessary. But notable critics, including Desmond MacCarthy and Edmund Wilson, have spoken in its defence as an important amplification of Joan's historical significance. Actresses playing the role have been similarly divided, as we may see from the accounts given in Holly Hill's book *Playing Joan: Actresses on the Challenge of Shaw's 'Saint Joan'* (Theatre Communications Group, New York 1987).

Anachronism

Anachronism is the introduction into the account of a particular historical period of elements that belong to another or others. Despite the fact that George Bernard Shaw insists upon the authenticity of his portrayal of the Middle Ages in *Saint Joan*, he uses anachronism tactically, to create dramatic effects. The boldest example comes in the Epilogue, where a churchman from the 1920s appears on stage to announce Joan's canonisation. This is an obvious violation of temporal unity, but it does bring the story up to date.

Use of the terms nationalism and Protestantism in Scene IV is also anachronistic, but it draws out Joan's full significance, for the benefit of contemporary audiences thoroughly familiar with those terms. George Bernard Shaw's use of modern idiom in the dialogue also serves his communicative purpose; he may be writing of the fifteenth century, but he is writing for the twentieth century. Anachronism can help disclose continuities between historical epochs, and so highlight the relevance of a distant era for our own.

THEMES

CREATIVE EVOLUTION AND THE LIFE FORCE

Although raised in a Protestant household, George Bernard Shaw lost his faith in Christianity while still in his teens. He did not believe in a paternal God, but he felt the need, nonetheless, for some principle of order and purpose in life. Like many intelligent individuals of his generation, he was fascinated by Charles Darwin's theory of evolution, outlined in *On the Origin of Species* (1859). The Christian sense of a loving God, whose grand design was manifest in the world, was replaced in Darwin's explanation by undirected change in the environment, requiring living creatures to adapt or perish. George Bernard Shaw found Darwinian purposelessness unpalatable, and he argued instead for 'Creative Evolution', a process in which the abilities and capacities of living beings become steadily more refined.

Drawing on the thinking of Samuel Butler, Arthur Schopenhauer, Friedrich Nietzsche and Henri Bergson, amongst others, he conceived in place of God, a Life Force. This impersonal 'great purpose' does not direct like a deity, nor does it intervene in human affairs, but works through those singularly receptive individuals, such as Saint Joan, who can perform appropriate actions towards the ultimate advancement of the species. Joan is different from other human beings, not in kind, but in the degree to which she is amenable to the influence of the Life Force; she becomes its agent, and in doing so alters the course of human history.

George Bernard Shaw developed the idea of Creative Evolution though his dramatic works, starting with *Man and Superman* (1903), and culminating with the cycle *Back to Methuselah* (1921).

HISTORICAL CHANGE

Joan was important to George Bernard Shaw because he felt she embodied the capacity of human beings to instigate changes within the historical development of societies. Her example as a prototype nationalist and Protestant had profound implications for the course of European history over the following centuries. George Bernard Shaw recognised positive advances in the strengthening of will that came with these changes. The capacity to envisage a future distinct in character from the present was one such advance, already well illustrated by Joan's independence of spirit. But there was much George Bernard Shaw disliked that also followed in the wake of nationalism and Protestantism. The capitalist economy, which was substantially nurtured by Protestantism, and which displaced the feudal system, George Bernard Shaw considered iniquitous. As a prominent socialist, he felt that further historical change was necessary to rectify the inequity and exploitation that seemed to him inherent in capitalism.

The terrible war fought in Europe between 1914 and 1918 may have been the full realisation of Joan's conception of serious combat, but it also seemed to George Bernard Shaw the ultimate proof of the need to pass beyond capitalist social organisation. Protestant individualism, which Joan dramatically foreshadowed, gave an enormous impetus to the historical epoch that followed, but George Bernard Shaw felt that the time had come for a revival of collective values, the next stage of European social development.

WOMEN'S RIGHTS

George Bernard Shaw rejected the conventional Victorian distinction between the characteristic qualities of men and of women. He believed that the sexes were essentially the same, and that the commonly recognised distinguishing features were the result of social conditioning. An evident aim of several of his plays was to inspire young women of the middle class to change their understanding of their role in the world. This change, he felt, would have repercussions through their families, and would contribute to an advance in middle-class thinking. This, in turn, would reverberate more extensively through social relationships. Joan's determination to dress like a man and to perform the work customarily done by men thus furnished an example which might challenge oppressive conditioning amongst George Bernard Shaw's contemporaries.

It is important to see George Bernard Shaw's belief in sexual equality as part of a larger set of convictions, rather than a cause he viewed in isolation. His was a socialist feminism. The feudal system against which Joan was reacting placed still more restrictive limits upon women than are experienced under capitalism. It is made clear in the play that in the Middle Ages, even more than in George Bernard Shaw's day, a middle-class woman's place was in the home.

PART FOUR

TEXTUAL ANALYSIS

TEXT 1 (SCENE IV, PAGES 98–9)

CAUCHON: Still you need not fear, my lord. Some men are born kings; and some are born statesmen. The two are seldom the same. Where would the king find counsellors to plan and carry out such a policy for him?

WARWICK [*with a not too friendly smile*]: Perhaps in the Church, my lord.

Cauchon, with an equally sour smile, shrugs his shoulders, and does not contradict him.

WARWICK: Strike down the barons; and the cardinals will have it all their own way.

CAUCHON [*conciliatory, dropping his polemical tone*]: My lord: we shall not defeat The Maid if we strive against one another. I know well that there is a Will to Power in the world. I know that while it lasts there will be a struggle between the Emperor and the Pope, between the dukes and the political cardinals, between the barons and the kings. The devil divides us and governs. I see you are no friend to The Church: you are an earl first and last, as I am a churchman first and last. But can we not sink our differences in the face of a common enemy? I see now that what is in your mind is not that this girl has never once mentioned The Church, and thinks only of God and herself, but that she has never once mentioned the peerage, and thinks only of the king and herself.

WARWICK: Quite so. These two ideas of hers are the same idea at bottom. It goes deep, my lord. It is the protest of the individual soul against the interference of priest or peer between the private man and his God. I should call it Protestantism if I had to find a name for it.

CAUCHON [*looking hard at him*]: You understand it wonderfully well, my lord. Scratch an Englishman, and find a Protestant.

WARWICK [*playing the pink of courtesy*]: I think you are not entirely void of sympathy with The Maid's secular heresy, my lord. I leave you to find a name for it.

CAUCHON: You mistake me, my lord. I have no sympathy with her political presumptions. But as a priest I have gained a knowledge of the minds of the common people; and there you will find yet another most dangerous idea. I can express it only by such phrases as France for the French, England for the English, Italy for the Italians, Spain for the Spanish, and so forth. It is sometimes so narrow and bitter in country folk that it surprises me that this country girl can rise above the idea of her village for its villagers. But she can. She does. When she threatens to drive the English from the soil of France she is undoubtedly thinking of the whole extent of country in which French is spoken. To her the French-speaking people are what the Holy Scriptures describe as a nation. Call this side of her heresy Nationalism if you will: I can find you no better name for it. I can only tell you that it is essentially anti-Catholic and anti-Christian; for the Catholic Church knows only one realm, and that is the realm of Christ's kingdom. Divide that kingdom into nations, and you dethrone Christ. Dethrone Christ, and who will stand between our throats and the sword? The world will perish in a welter of war.

This passage is taken from Scene IV, the only scene in the play where Joan does not appear at all. Significantly, it shows the development of ideas, abstract notions of the kind Joan avoids, preferring to engage in direct action. In this extract we see Bishop Cauchon engaged in dialogue with the Earl of Warwick. George Bernard Shaw uses their conversation to delineate the momentous changes in social organisation and religious belief heralded by Joan's unorthodox attitudes.

The French bishop is welcomed in the English camp in a way unthinkable in the conduct of modern warfare. George Bernard Shaw wishes to indicate the view of social relationships prevailing during the Middle Ages, and to stress that, whatever their differences, Cauchon and Warwick recognise a common enemy in the Maid of Orleans.

The earl has been articulating his fear that the feudal system will crumble if Joan has her way. Her intention is to invest power in the new king, and that will divest the feudal lords of their enormous influence. In medieval Europe, monarchs were largely figureheads, while aristocrats owned property and held sway. If the king became an actual ruler rather than just a symbol of authority, Warwick and members of his class would suffer immeasurable losses. The peasantry and other members of the lower classes, currently dependent upon their lords, would find themselves elevated accordingly.

His vision has in fact been realised, for this is the course that European history has taken. Here, however, Cauchon offers consolation on the grounds that, 'Some men are born kings; and some are born statesmen. The two are seldom the same.' His point is that those who find themselves in positions of social power rarely have the ability to fulfil the potential of those privileged positions. In consequence, they invariably need to rely upon shrewd political manipulators, such as Warwick. His kind will remain, the bishop argues, the real power behind the throne. George Bernard Shaw shared this view of the practical inadequacy of most leaders. Partly as a consequence of this he was impressed by the rise of contemporary figures such as Mussolini in Italy, and Hitler in Germany. At times his admiration for the efficiency of Fascism as a social programme blinded him to the ethical failings of that political system of rule through force.

Medieval Catholicism aspired to be the universal Church, embracing all human beings. Warwick would necessarily have been a member of it, but his outlook is notably secular rather than spiritual. He suggests that the power vacuum which would follow the displacement of the feudal lords might be filled by cardinals. He evidently regards these representatives of the Church as rivals rather than allies. Cauchon, however, emphasises the need to preserve an alliance against the driving force of Joan's vision. Cauchon speaks, in terms which for George Bernard Shaw's contemporaries would recall the philosopher Friedrich Nietzsche (1844–1900), of a 'Will to Power' at work in the world. He is acknowledging the realities of political rivalry and of the manoeuvring it entails, and is admitting that the head of his Church, the pope, has to address those realities as much as the secular emperor. He does not deny their divisions, but he advocates a pragmatic settling of differences to allow concerted action against the common enemy. Secular and spiritual interests both face a genuine threat from Joan.

Warwick then gives expression to George Bernard Shaw's view that Joan was the prototype Protestant: 'It is the protest of the individual soul against the interference of priest or peer between the private man and his God. I should call it Protestantism if I had to find a name for it.' Historically, the Protestant spirit took root far more effectively in England than in France. Arguably, it was that inclination to unfettered independent thought that promoted the dynamic ethos of capitalism in English society. The particular nature of capitalist organisation in England spawned an Industrial Revolution; France, which remained predominantly Catholic, for a long time clung more tenaciously to a largely rural economy, based in agriculture.

The two nations, at the time so closely linked, were to develop along rather different lines. The bishop seems to predict this with his wry comment: 'Scratch an Englishman, and find a Protestant.' This prompts Warwick to suggest that in his ready recognition of a distinct national character Cauchon seems ready to espouse the 'secular heresy' promoted by Joan. The bishop distances himself from this 'dangerous idea', to which he gives the name nationalism. He observes that the international system of feudalism is not alone in needing to fear this phenomenon: the universal aspirations of the Church are also jeopardised by its emergence. The spread of nationalism will, he predicts, 'dethrone Christ' and the consequence will be 'a welter of war'. The prediction would have been especially resonant for audiences in the years following the First World War, fought between 1914 and 1918.

We can see here that George Bernard Shaw is certainly not simplistically associating Joan with good and her opponents with evil. Cauchon is a pious man; Warwick is more ruthless. But it is Joan who helps bring into the world Protestantism and nationalism, which will transform it. George Bernard Shaw saw material and spiritual advances derived from these innovations, but he also saw the First World War as their culmination, as a momentous sign of the need to move on to the next evolutionary stage. Collective values and international understanding had their place in the world once again, he felt. Their refinement would involve significant advance upon the Middle Ages, and would take on board lessons to be learned from the historical phase that Joan may be said to have initiated.

TEXT 2 (SCENE VI, PAGES 128–9)

COURCELLES: Your lordship is merciful, of course. But it is a great responsibility to depart from the usual practice.

JOAN: Thou art a rare noodle, Master. Do what was done last time is thy rule, eh?

COURCELLES [*rising*]: Thou wanton: dost thou dare call me noodle?

THE INQUISITOR: Patience, Master, patience: I fear you will soon be only too terribly avenged.

COURCELLES [*mutters*]: Noodle indeed! [*He sits down, much discontented*].

THE INQUISITOR: Meanwhile, let us not be moved by the rough side of a shepherd lass's tongue.

JOAN: Nay: I am no shepherd lass, though I have helped with the sheep like anyone else. I will do a lady's work in the house – spin or weave – against any woman in Rouen.

THE INQUISITOR: This is not a time for vanity, Joan. You stand in great peril.

JOAN: I know it: have I not been punished for my vanity? If I had not worn my cloth of gold surcoat in battle like a fool, that Burgundian soldier would never have pulled me backwards off my horse; and I should not have been here.

THE CHAPLAIN: If you are so clever at woman's work why do you not stay at home and do it?

JOAN: There are plenty of other women to do it; but there is nobody to do my work.

CAUCHON: Come! we are wasting time on trifles. Joan: I am going to put a most solemn question to you. Take care how you answer; for your life and salvation are at stake on it. Will you for all you have said and done, be it good or bad, accept the judgment of God's Church on earth? More especially as to the acts and words that are imputed to you in this trial by the Promoter here, will you submit your case to the inspired interpretation of the Church Militant?

JOAN: I am a faithful child of the Church. I will obey the Church –

CAUCHON [*hopefully leaning forward*]: You will?

JOAN: – provided it does not command anything impossible.

Cauchon sinks back in his chair with a heavy sigh. The Inquisitor purses his lips and frowns. Ladvenu shakes his head pitifully.

D'ESTIVET: She imputes to the Church the error and folly of commanding the impossible.

JOAN: If you command me to declare that all that I have done and said, and all the visions and revelations I have had, were not from God, then that is impossible: I will not declare it for anything in the world. What God made me do I will never go back on; and what He has commanded or shall command I will not fail to do in spite of any man alive. That is what I mean by impossible. And in case the Church should bid me do anything contrary to the command I have from God, I will not consent to it, no matter what it may be.

THE ASSESSORS [*shocked and indignant*]: Oh! The Church contrary to God! What do you say now? Flat heresy. This is beyond everything, etc., etc.

D'ESTIVET [*throwing down his brief*]: My lord: do you need anything more than this?

CAUCHON: Woman: you have said enough to burn ten heretics. Will you not be warned? Will you not understand?

THE INQUISITOR: If the Church Militant tells you that your revelations and visions are sent by the devil to tempt you to your damnation, will you not believe that the Church is wiser than you?

JOAN: I believe that God is wiser than I; and it is His commands that I will do.

The play's opening scenes are dominated by action, and by Joan's passionate concern for what the future holds. In Scene VI, the trial forms a largely static environment, and emphasis falls on interpretation of the recent past. Underneath the dialogue, however, the course of historical events is still unfolding, and the court is, in effect, the platform that will launch Joan's historical reputation.

Canon de Courcelles is an earnest young priest who is devoted to precedent, and abhors departure from the way things have been done in the past. He has been advocating torture to extract confession from the young woman. Modern audiences might regard him as a sadistic figure, but Courcelles merely argues that such treatment of prisoners is customary. Joan is here scornful of his devotion to tradition and the example of the past. She is a rebel, and shows no respect for the authority of past practices. George Bernard Shaw shared her sense that worship of tradition was an impediment to be overcome in the cause of human advancement. It is possible that early audiences may have perceived a connection between this imprisoned young woman, threatened with brutal treatment, and the suffragettes whose male captors had recently subjected them to such brutal indignities as forced feeding.

The campaigners for suffrage were also in conflict with the defenders of traditional ways.

Joan's informal mode of address is carried into the courtroom. In this context her impishness comes over as reckless impertinence. Calling Courcelles 'a rare noodle' is a way of brandishing her indifference to the authority that he holds in such esteem. George Bernard Shaw has used Joan's familiar idiom as a means to make her attractive to audiences, but a show of respect would undoubtedly have been more diplomatic at this point, with her life at stake. The fact is that Joan is not temperamentally inclined to pause for thought; hers is an active rather than a reflective character, and her dynamism inevitably creates enemies amongst those who would prefer to preserve the old ways.

Courcelles's pride, which produces his angry response to Joan's insult, appears trivial besides Joan's pride, which is not selfish in a narrowly egotistical sense, but is bound inextricably to her understanding that she must perform God's will. The canon's pique seems small-minded and mean-spirited compared to Joan's expansiveness. Her alleged vanity becomes an issue in the court, however, when the Inquisitor, seeking to console Courcelles, describes her dismissively as a shepherd lass. Her response indicates that she belongs to a more elevated social class. George Bernard Shaw wished to rectify the misconception that Joan was a simple peasant girl, partly because he wished to show social change being driven by a representative of the middle ranks of society. He was keenly aware that those ranks furnished the majority of the audience for his plays. It was to them above all that he spoke, and to them that he looked for a practical response in changing social attitudes and behaviour.

Medieval France was a patriarchal society. It was ruled by men, and the role of women was closely circumscribed. Joan refers to the work performed by a lady – spinning and weaving. Daring to move beyond those domestic tasks, Joan was vulnerable to what George Bernard Shaw called 'Anti-Feminist' reprisals. His view was that the unjust patriarchy had remained more or less in place, despite the changing appearance of social relationships. *Saint Joan* can be seen as an instance of the support he voiced for the cause of women's rights.

The discussion of the young woman's vanity highlights two distinct interpretations, within this Christian country, of the individual's relationship to God. Joan conceives vanity in terms of outward trappings, and points out that her capture followed her adoption of a 'cloth of gold surcoat' as battledress. Protestantism would later denounce all such ornamentation. The Catholic court, on the other hand, steeped in ritual and symbolism, sees vanity in Joan's self-esteem, which accepts no limits from institution or custom. George Bernard Shaw wished both points of view to be respected as historical realities within an ongoing evolutionary process. Joan was being true to her beliefs, but so were the members of the court. The divergence evident in their dialogue cannot be resolved; it discloses two distinct and irreconcilable world-views.

The body language of Cauchon, the Inquisitor and Ladvenu, outlined in George Bernard Shaw's stage directions, shows their genuine concern for the fate of Joan's soul. They are not bent on vengeance, but wish to see her restored to the path of salvation, from which, in their view, she has departed. As representatives of the Church Militant, the Church on earth, they are obliged to respond to her apparently heretical behaviour. Joan, however, persists in her total faith in direct revelation from God to the individual.

Medieval Catholicism's emphasis was collective; Reformation Protestantism involved a radical shift to the individual. As a socialist, George Bernard Shaw felt the need for a renewal of collective interest, drawing benefit from the lessons learned during the individualist phase. His philosophy of Creative Evolution enabled him to envisage a subsequent renewal of individualism, in turn refined by the advances made by the new collectivism (see Theme on Creative Evolution and The Life Force).

TEXT 3 (EPILOGUE, PAGES 148–9)

JOAN [*laughing heartily*]: Ha ha! I was no beauty: I was always a rough one: a regular soldier. I might almost as well have been a man. Pity I wasnt: I should not have bothered you all so much then. But my head was in the skies; and the glory of God was upon me; and, man or woman, I should have bothered you as long as your noses were in the mud. Now tell me what has happened since you wise men knew no better than to make a heap of cinders of me?

CHARLES: Your mother and brothers have sued the courts to have your case tried over again. And the courts have declared that your judges were full of corruption and cozenage, fraud and malice.

JOAN: Not they. They were as honest a lot of poor fools as ever burned their betters.

CHARLES: The sentence on you is broken, annihilated, annulled: null, non-existent, without value or effect.

JOAN: I was burned, all the same. Can they unburn me?

CHARLES: If they could, they would think twice before they did it. But they have decreed that a beautiful cross be placed where the stake stood, for your perpetual memory and for your salvation.

JOAN: It is the memory and the salvation that sanctify the cross, not the cross that sanctifies the memory and the salvation. [*She turns away, forgetting him*] I shall outlast that cross. I shall be remembered when men will have forgotten where Rouen stood.

CHARLES: There you go with your self-conceit, the same as ever! I think you might say a word of thanks to me for having had justice done at last.

CAUCHON [*appearing at the window between them*]: Liar!

CHARLES: Thank you.

JOAN: Why, if it isnt Peter Cauchon! How are you, Peter? What luck have you had since you burned me?

CAUCHON: None. I arraign the justice of Man. It is not the justice of God.

JOAN: Still dreaming of justice, Peter? See what justice came to with me! But what has happened to thee? Art dead or alive?

CAUCHON: Dead. Dishonored. They pursued me beyond the grave. They excommunicated my dead body: they dug it up and flung it into the common sewer.

JOAN: Your dead body did not feel the spade and the sewer as my live body felt the fire.

CAUCHON: But this thing that they have done against me hurts justice; destroys faith; saps the foundation of the Church. The solid earth sways like the treacherous sea beneath the feet of men and spirits alike when the innocent are slain in the name of law, and their wrongs are undone by slandering the pure of heart.

JOAN: Well, well, Peter, I hope men will be the better for remembering me; and they would not remember me so well if you had not burned me.

CAUCHON: They will be the worse for remembering me: they will see in me evil triumphing over good, falsehood over truth, cruelty over mercy, hell over heaven. Their courage will rise as they think of you, only to faint as they think of me. Yet God is my witness I was just: I was merciful: I was faithful to my light: I could do no other than I did.

This excerpt is taken from the Epilogue, that section of the play which some critics have found unsatisfactory on account of its departure from the play's predominantly realistic mode. The scene takes the form of a waking dream, with Joan's ghost visiting the chamber of the king. But George Bernard Shaw was keen to stress that Joan's real story began with her death. At that point she departed from medieval France and took her place on the stage of European history. The Epilogue is thus a startling device to prevent audiences consigning Joan's significance to the realm of the past; her relevance, he insists, is ongoing.

George Bernard Shaw's Joan is robust as a ghost, as she was in life. Here we see her laughing, heartily yet without malice. Her basic humanity is highlighted through her sense of humour, and she laughs at herself, showing that although she possesses enormous self-assurance she is not a shallow egotist. In his Preface, George Bernard Shaw insists that Joan was a physically plain woman; it was not facile sexual allure that led men to follow her. Joan shows herself to be under no misapprehension about her looks, but such a superficial matter causes her no distress. She has had more serious issues to attend to.

There is perspicacity in her recognition that had she been a man there would have been far less controversy surrounding her behaviour. Exclusion of women from the realm of action is one of the key areas that George Bernard Shaw seeks to address and help rectify through his play.

Charles is mocked as a representative of conventional wisdom, but the wise men who condemned Joan were necessarily constrained by the limits of their understanding. Joan was forcing a way through those limits, driven by sheer energy, rather than intellectual calculation. The magnanimity with which she regards, in retrospect, her own execution indicates the confidence she has in her historical destiny. She has transcended the 'heap of cinders' she became. In that transcendence, however, she has retained her down-to-earth idiom.

The king is able to tell Joan of her family's efforts to clear her name, and to have her judges condemned as corrupt. Joan's reputation actually underwent such a process of rehabilitation, which succeeded largely on account of the political necessity of validating the coronation of Charles VII. As long as the king could be said to have gained power as a result of witchcraft, or the actions of a heretic, his position remained insecure. This should be borne in mind when he suggests that Joan might thank him 'for having had justice done at last'.

Joan, however, while ready to concede that her judges were fools, defends their honesty in conducting the trial according to an established sense of justice. Charles observes that the authorities who have annulled her sentence would be less than keen to see this troublesome woman alive again. The annulment is expedient, but Joan is still regarded with trepidation by the male ruling class. This observation is given dramatic form at the end of the Epilogue, when the prospect of her resurrection, and of the turbulence that might follow it, fills the men on stage with horror. De Stogumber then pleads, 'Oh, do not come back: you must not come back' (p. 158).

It is **ironic** that the Catholic Church has erected a cross to mark Joan's memory, and to assist her salvation so soon after adjudging her a heretic. The irony is underlined by her declaration that 'It is the memory and the salvation that sanctify the cross, not the cross that sanctifies the memory and the salvation.' This is a quintessentially Protestant utterance, playing down the importance of the religious symbol and stressing the significance of the individual's state of faith.

Joan's visionary nature is such that she can imagine a time when memory of Rouen itself will have faded, yet her own reputation will persist. Charles accuses her of conceitedness, but what appears to others to be arrogance is actually profound self-assurance, drawing its strength from faith and imagination. Absence of self-doubt is a great enabling factor in Joan's character, allowing her to achieve her goals without debilitating anxiety or uncertainty.

The difference in perspective between Joan and the king is emphasised when Cauchon's ghost appears on stage between them. Joan extends a warm welcome to the bishop who helped condemn her to burn. Characteristically informal, she calls him Peter, choosing to address the man rather than show conventional reverence for his office.

Cauchon declares, 'I arraign the justice of Man.' The word 'arraign' is a judicial term, signalling the summoning of a prisoner to court to have charges read. The bishop is still seeking to act as a judge, and he remains devoted to God's justice, which in his view has been travestied in human courts. He clearly has in mind the court that overturned his own judgement, rehabilitating Joan, and bringing ignominy upon his own reputation.

He, in turn, became a victim: 'They excommunicated my dead body: they dug it up and flung it into the common sewer.' This is a grotesque illustration of the wild swings to which human judgement is susceptible. The purposeful course of Joan's life appears remarkably straight and steadfast by comparison. It is clear from his words that Cauchon, despite the indignities suffered by his corpse, sustains his faith in the Church and in God's justice, which he represented. George Bernard Shaw continues to stress that the bishop acted in good faith, and was not the corrupt, vindictive figure portrayed by some historians.

Joan seeks to console him: 'Well, well, Peter, I hope men will be the better for remembering me; and they would not remember me so well if you had not burned me.' It is tempting to recognise here a conscious echo of the Christian argument for the 'Fortunate Fall'. This holds that the expulsion from Eden may retrospectively be considered a happy event, as it enabled human beings to know redemption through Jesus Christ. Christ's crucifixion became the occasion of salvation. Cauchon, like Pontius Pilate, has been cast as the villainous judge, whose condemnatory judgement was actually a necessary component of God's design.

Cauchon is not reconciled to this fate. He recognises that denigration of his judgement in fact undermines the authority of the Catholic Church. Joan has triumphed over him, and this foreshadows a more general threat to his entire world-view posed by the ascendancy of Protestant belief. The artifice of this Epilogue breaks the logic of realistic representation, but it enables George Bernard Shaw to draw out further the significance of Joan's position on the stage of history.

PART FIVE

BACKGROUND

GEORGE BERNARD SHAW

George Bernard Shaw was born in Dublin, on 26 July 1856, but spent most of his adult life in England. His father, George Carr Shaw was a grain merchant; his mother, Lucinda Gurley, who came from a landowning family, was a singer. The couple already had two daughters, Lucinda and Elinor. The Shaws were Irish Protestants living in a predominantly Catholic community, so an awareness of those religious differences that feature prominently in *Saint Joan* was an integral part of his early life.

In 1871, he left school and worked as a clerk in a land agent's office. Two years later, his mother left her alcoholic husband and moved with her daughters to London. Her son joined them there in 1876. George Bernard Shaw then embarked on a programme of self-education, using the facilities offered by the British Museum, and participating in the lively and wide-ranging discussions of debating societies. At the same time, he started writing fiction. This resulted in the publication of five novels.

In 1882, George Bernard Shaw attended a lecture by Henry George, American author of *Progress and Poverty*, and he became an ardent socialist. He started reading the work of philosopher Karl Marx, and found it stimulating, although he was wary of Marxism's revolutionary turbulence. As a member of the Marxist Social Democratic League, he became acquainted with Marx's daughter Eleanor (1855–98), and with the distinguished English socialist, William Morris (1834–96).

Then, in 1884, he joined the recently formed Fabian Society, a predominantly middle-class group of intellectuals, dedicated to the reform of society through constitutional means according to Democratic Socialist principles. Amongst his closest friends in the movement were Beatrice Webb (1858–1943) and her husband Sidney (1859–1947), founders of the London School of Economics, and of the journal *The New Statesman*.

As a leading member of the Fabians, George Bernard Shaw travelled widely in England, delivering lectures that advocated socialist reform. He wrote copiously on behalf of the group, producing many pamphlets. In 1889, he edited and contributed two essays to *Fabian Essays in Socialism*. In 1900, in response to the Boer War in South Africa, he published *Fabianism and the Empire*. In time, his liberal optimism waned, and was increasingly supplanted by his philosophy of the Life Force. Some of his more extreme political declarations, formulated under the aegis of this philosophy, were met with unequivocal disapproval in Fabian circles.

From the mid 1880s George Bernard Shaw made a living as a journalist, writing criticism of art, music and literature for a variety of journals and newspapers. He was drama critic for *The Saturday Review* between 1895 and 1898. This experience honed his awareness of dramatic techniques, and also alerted him to the limitations of many of the fashionable plays of the day.

In 1896, George Bernard Shaw met Charlotte Payne-Townshend, a wealthy Irish socialist, who became his wife in 1898. In 1906, the couple moved from London to the village of Ayot St Lawrence, in Hertfordshire. Meanwhile, his plays were establishing his reputation as a major writer. They were also highly successful in commercial terms. Some of his best-known works, including *Major Barbara* (1905), *The Doctor's Dilemma* (1906) and *Pygmalion* (1914), belong to this period.

In 1914, following the outbreak of the First World War, George Bernard Shaw published *Common Sense About the War*. At a time when his popularity was at its height, his criticism of British leaders and their conduct of the war generated an intensely hostile response from the public, leaving him hugely unpopular for some time. *Heartbreak House* (1919), one of his most accomplished plays, channelled his fears and anxieties about the conflict into **symbolic** dramatic form. He modified his views in support of the war effort, and in 1917 took up an invitation to make an official visit to the Western Front, in Flanders.

Saint Joan (1923) restored George Bernard Shaw to popular esteem. In 1925, his literary reputation reached its zenith, when he was awarded the Nobel Prize for literature. He requested that the money attached to the award should be used to stage plays by the controversial Swedish dramatist, August Strindberg (1849–1912), whose work he greatly admired.

In 1929, Sir Barry Jackson established the Malvern Festival, dedicated to performances of George Bernard Shaw's plays and the music of Sir Edward Elgar. In 1931, George Bernard Shaw was invited to Moscow, where he met Joseph Stalin, the Soviet leader. His praise for Soviet achievement, and his enthusiasm for Stalin and for the Fascist leaders Mussolini in Italy and Hitler in Germany, led once again to a period during which he was out of favour in Britain.

George Bernard Shaw's wife Charlotte died in 1943. He himself died on 2 November 1950. Following cremation, his ashes were scattered in the garden of his home, around a statue of Saint Joan erected by his neighbour, the sculptress Clara Winston.

The adjective 'Shavian', derived from his name, has entered the language to connote a characteristic form of wit.

The standard biography is Michael Holroyd's monumental *Bernard Shaw*, 3 volumes (Random House, 1988). A thorough, and at times startling examination of George Bernard Shaw's political thought is offered by Gareth Griffith's *Socialism and Superior Brains* (Routledge, 1993).

His other works

George Bernard Shaw wrote a great deal during his long life. His first play was *Widowers' Houses* (1892), an exposé of slums and their landlords, and an early indication of his opposition to capitalist social organisation, with its inherent division between the very wealthy and the poor. *Mrs Warren's Profession* (1898), which followed, is a play reflecting the radical spirit of Ibsen. It addresses the issue of prostitution, and was initially banned, not being performed until 1902. Both plays show a determination to confront important social issues of the day in a frank and critical manner.

It was his skill as a writer of comedies, however, that enabled George Bernard Shaw to win a popular audience for his work, starting with *Arms and the Man* (1894). Even at his most elegantly witty, George Bernard Shaw sought to convey a serious message. He was shrewd enough to realise that humour could be used tactically to communicate with people habitually resistant to the preaching of political educators.

He was also aware of a taste for historical drama amongst contemporary theatregoers, and had made several forays into that territory before writing *Saint Joan*. For example, in *The Man of Destiny* (1898) he took Napoleon, with whom Joan is compared in the Preface to *Saint Joan*, as his hero. George Bernard Shaw grouped *Saint Joan* with *Caesar and Cleopatra* (1901) as a **chronicle play**. The term suggests faithful adherence to the record of a sequence of actual events. Indeed, George Bernard Shaw wryly asserted that, 'Familiarity with them would get a student safely though examination papers on their periods'. This should not be allowed to obscure the fact that George Bernard Shaw's historical reconstructions invariably illustrate highly personal concerns, and can scarcely be taken as objective records.

George Bernard Shaw's philosophy of the Life Force was initially outlined in *Man and Superman* (1903). A more detailed account of that philosophy and of his belief in Creative Evolution appeared in *Back to Methuselah* (1921).

HISTORICAL BACKGROUND

THE HUNDRED YEARS WAR

England and France were at war intermittently between 1337 and 1453. Although the conflict was by no means continuous, skirmishes occurred with sufficient regularity for historians to call it the Hundred Years War.

In 1337, Edward III of England lay claim to the French throne. In 1346, his forces defeated the French at Crécy, and captured the port of Calais. In 1356, the Black Prince, Edward's son, won a victory at Poitiers, and imprisoned John II of France. Settlements were reached, and for a while relations between the two countries were relatively stable.

Then, in 1415, Henry V invaded France, renewing the English claim. He won a famous victory at Agincourt. By the Treaty of Troyes, implemented in 1420, the French throne was to pass from Charles VI to the heir of Henry V. The Dauphin, later Charles VII, was declared illegitimate, and so barred from succession. When Charles VI and Henry V both died in 1422, Henry VI was still a minor, and the Dauphin soon entered into dispute over his right to become king. Six years after his father's death, the Dauphin remained uncrowned, while the army of Henry VI, supported by the feudal lords of Burgundy, occupied the northern part of France. Rheims, where coronations were staged, fell within that occupied territory.

At this point, Joan of Arc arrived on the scene. In 1428, the English forces lay siege to Orleans. Her role in lifting that siege proved a crucial turning point, and Charles VII was crowned at Rheims Cathedral in July 1429. By the time he died, in 1461, the English had been driven from France.

Joan of Arc

Joan was born around 1412 at Domrémy, between Champagne and Lorraine. At the age of thirteen, she began hearing voices, and seeing visions of Saint Catherine, Saint Margaret and Saint Michael. In May 1428, and again in January 1429 she journeyed to Vaucouleurs, seeking authorisation to join the Dauphin at Chinon. She led the Dauphin's troops to Orleans, and early in May 1429 lifted the siege. Further significant victories followed, and in July she was invited to attend the coronation of Charles VII.

In May 1430, she was captured by soldiers of the Duke of Burgundy, who was an ally of the English invaders. She was handed over to the Bishop of Beauvais upon payment of ten thousand francs. She was tried at Rouen, at the end of March 1431. On 23 May, she was told to renounce her heretical ways or face punishment from the secular authorities. The following day she signed a form declaring that she repudiated her heresies. Within a few days she was considered to have relapsed, and she was condemned to be burnt at the stake. Her execution took place on 30 May 1431.

In 1450, Charles VII, whose kingship had been secured by Joan, and who was keen to establish the validity of his rule, ordered an investigation into the trial. In 1456, the pope annulled the sentence passed on her in 1431. She was canonised by Pope Benedict XV on 16 May 1920.

George Bernard Shaw claimed that writing this play involved transcription of the historical facts, and indicated that the trial scene was taken directly from a contemporary account. There is considerable documentation extant from that 1431 trial, and from the rehabilitation proceedings of 1456. Nonetheless, his account required a lot of information to be distilled into a limited space, and the extent of George Bernard Shaw's creative intervention should not be underestimated.

An account of Saint Joan's life can be found in Regine Pernoud's *Joan of Arc* (Penguin, 1969).

THE FEUDAL SYSTEM

The European feudal system developed during the eighth century, and flourished between the tenth and the thirteenth centuries. Feudal lords held land in 'fief' from the king in return for their allegiance, which included military support. The feudal lord's estate was the key social, administrative and economic unit during the Middle Ages. The land was distributed amongst the peasantry for cultivation and pasturage, in return for labour and a percentage of agricultural produce. The lord also levied taxes, and could press his serfs into military service. As the Earl of Warwick points out in George Bernard Shaw's play, the aristocracy was the real seat of power in medieval society, and class allegiance was stronger than national boundaries. So, the Duke of Burgundy entered into alliance with the invading English, whereas at a later date he would surely have felt obliged to serve the French nation.

In Joan of Arc's day, the dominance of feudalism was being eroded by a number of factors. Unlike capitalism which superseded it, the feudal economy was largely static, changing little over long periods. But the system of manorial estates developed inefficiencies that caused financial problems. The emergent merchant class increasingly challenged the aristocracy when their interests clashed. As the economy changed, so did the political system. The nation state ruled by a powerful monarch came to supplant the old order, and lower and upper classes both became subjects of their sovereign. As the play suggests, the English, living on an island, were especially ready to espouse the new nationalism, which subsequently took hold in continental Europe. George Bernard Shaw presents Joan as the embodiment of this radical new spirit.

The medieval Church was closely integrated with the feudal system. It derived great wealth from its own estates, drawing revenue from tenants. The relationship of the Earl of Warwick and Bishop Cauchon in *Saint Joan* is indicative of the kind of relationship that existed between wielders of secular and of religious power. The Church exercised additional power through its close regulation of culture, controlling the availability of education and the acquisition of literacy. George Bernard Shaw reflects this facet of cultural power in his play.

During the nineteenth century, writers such as William Morris (1834–96) and John Ruskin (1819–1900) had revived interest in medieval civilisation, and George Bernard Shaw felt that in *Saint Joan* he was continuing their work. But he was showing in the play the beginning of the end for that epoch, with Joan's prototypal nationalism and Protestantism heralding the end of the old internationalist order. George Bernard Shaw depicts the initiation of that phase of history traced in Johan Huizinga's classic study *The Waning of the Middle Ages* (Pelican Books, 1972), first published, coincidentally, in 1924. George Bernard Shaw would not have known this book while writing his play, but it is evidence of a more general interest amongst his contemporaries in the transition from medieval to modern societies.

THE INQUISITION

The Inquisition was set up by Pope Gregory IX in 1231, in order to combat heresy. It was especially militant and powerful in the south of France, and in northern Italy, during the thirteenth and fourteenth centuries. The use of torture to obtain confessions was authorised in 1252, although the most severe penalty it could impose was life imprisonment. Proven heretics were handed over to the secular authorities to administer fit punishment. The fate of Joan illustrates this policy.

Towards the end of the fifteenth century, the Inquisition was instituted in Spain, where it operated with notorious cruelty. That phase of the Inquisition's history is the one usually evoked today by mention of its name.

THE FIRST WORLD WAR

The First World War (1914–18) cast a long shadow across George Bernard Shaw's view of human beings. The extent of human slaughter at battles such as Ypres and the Somme was unprecedented, and the role of new technologies gave this mechanised conflict a profoundly dehumanising character. He found it increasingly difficult to register an optimistic tone, and his humour grew more sardonic through plays such as *Heartbreak House* (1919) and *Back to Methuselah* (1921). Increasingly it was in the exceptional individual rather than the majority that his faith in human advancement lay. This shift in his sensibility inclined him more to the writing of tragic drama than to the comedies that had earlier made his name.

Joan embodies a shift from archaic to modern methods of conducting war, so the cataclysm of the First World War can in a sense be regarded as her ultimate legacy. This appears particularly to be the case as the war was fought across France and Belgium over nationalistic issues, and George Bernard Shaw's Joan is the first nationalist. George Bernard Shaw's enthusiasm for Joan did not blind him to the disasters following from her example; the evolutionary process, in his view, was not unalloyed progress, but involved human catastrophes as well as major gains. George Bernard Shaw felt that a further evolutionary stage was necessary to move human beings out of the capitalist system which, as a socialist, he considered iniquitously ruthless in its exploitation of human resources. The First World War was, he recognised, a climactic point in the history of European capitalism.

IRISH NATIONALISM

George Bernard Shaw left Ireland in 1876, and it was three decades before he returned to his native land. His plays contain very little direct reference to Irish issues, although he did write regular journalistic pieces dealing with Ireland's political difficulties. He became particularly engaged with the question of Ulster's future, following the passing of the Home Rule Act in 1914.

Then, in 1916, Roger Casement, a fellow Irishman, was put on trial as a German agent who had tried to foment revolution against British rule in Ireland. In time of war, this was perceived by the government as an unequivocal act of treason, but George Bernard Shaw drafted a speech for the accused man, claiming that he was in fact a prisoner of war. Casement delivered the speech, but was subsequently hanged.

George Bernard Shaw had earlier in that year argued for prisoner-of-war status for the leaders of the Easter Rising in Dublin, a concerted action intended to overthrow rule from Westminster. Although he considered the Rising an untenable romantic adventure, George Bernard Shaw declared that as an Irishman he felt any action taken to move towards Irish independence was entirely justified. He considered the execution barbaric.

In November 1917, George Bernard Shaw published the prosaically entitled pamphlet, *How to Settle the Irish Question*. It would be a mistake to see him as an unequivocal supporter of the nationalist cause. His Protestant upbringing complicated his relationship with the predominantly Catholic supporters of Irish nationalism. Moreover, he considered the insular nature of much nationalistic thinking to be undesirable, and felt that nationalist consciousness needed eventually to be subordinated to a more general sense of shared human aspiration.

In 1920, while violence flared, he drafted for the Labour Party a report, *Irish Nationalism and Labour Internationalism*, which stressed the need to establish socialist solidarity across national boundaries. In fact the Government of Ireland Act, passed in that year, divided the country into two self-governing areas. The Parliament of Northern Ireland, in Belfast, was opened in 1921. The Irish Free State was established in 1922.

Saint Joan's wish to see English soldiers driven from her native land would seem to correspond in broad terms to the dramatist's response to the legacy of colonialism in Ireland. Her execution offers a parallel to that of Patrick Pearse and other Republican leaders of the 1916 Rising.

THE RUSSIAN REVOLUTION

In 1917, Nicholas II, the Tsar of Russia, was overthrown by Bolshevik forces, led by Lenin. George Bernard Shaw declared himself a communist and welcomed the revolution, supporting Lenin's ruthless methods in establishing his new order. In this he differed from many fellow Fabians, and indeed from some leading British Marxists. Upheaval in the nature of government was a crucial topic of the day, so the changes wrought by Joan could be seen to have pressing contemporary relevance.

THE FABIAN SOCIETY

The Fabian Society was a group composed of predominantly middle-class socialists. Their political views focused on the need for collective responsibility, ensuring the welfare of all members of society through the efforts of all members of society. They avoided the revolutionary radicalism advocated by Karl Marx (1818–83), aiming to secure change through intellectual persuasion rather than violent mass action of the kind that had brought the Soviet Union into existence.

George Bernard Shaw's espousal of the Life Force eventually weakened his faith in the efficacy of democratic procedures, and compromised his involvement with Fabian politics and their liberal tenets.

CONTEMPORARY FEMINISM

In 1903, Emmeline Pankhurst established the Women's Social and Political Union (WSPU), an organisation committed to the extension to women of the right to vote. George Bernard Shaw had voiced support for such broadening of suffrage back in 1884, in a *Manifesto* written for the Fabian Society. His relationship with Pankhurst's group was, however, characteristically complex, resulting in occasional disharmony. Nonetheless, given the importance George Bernard Shaw placed on young women of the middle class as especially receptive members of his audience, the Union was an important sign that action for change was under way.

Mass rallies were staged, and there were highly visible protests, including women chaining themselves to railings in public places. The activity proved so effectively unsettling that in 1913 the government passed a repressive Act, known as the 'Cat and Mouse Act', to counter militant feminist agitation. In prison, many of the 'Suffragettes' were subjected to the indignities of force-feeding. George Bernard Shaw believed that women should use their own voices, rather than have him speak on their behalf, but he remained a prominent supporter of women's emancipation. This is evident in his characterisation of Joan.

During the First World War, women entered areas of employment vacated by men who were caught up in the fighting. They also served in non-combative roles, working in munitions factories at home, and acting as nurses and ambulance drivers at the front. Joan's refusal to be confined to domestic employment had topical significance.

In 1931, in the course of a radio broadcast marking the five-hundredth anniversary of Joan's execution, George Bernard Shaw directly compared Joan to Sylvia Pankhurst, militant daughter of the founder of the WSPU.

THE CANONISATION OF SAINT JOAN

Saint Joan was written in 1923. Joan of Arc had been canonised by the Vatican only in 1920. George Bernard Shaw's characterisation of Joan as a down-to-earth rebel goes against the stereotypical notion that saints are ethereal beings. But he was not concerned to show her as an orthodox religious figure; rather, he seized the opportunity to employ an appealing historical individual, who was very much in the public eye, in order to pursue arguments that were particularly important to him.

LITERARY BACKGROUND

EARLIER LITERARY VERSIONS OF SAINT JOAN

George Bernard Shaw was critical of Shakespeare's portrayal of Joan in *Henry VI, Part I*. He argued that Shakespeare had failed to create a medieval Joan, seeing her squarely through the lens of the Renaissance, the subsequent phase of European cultural history. In his Preface, George Bernard Shaw discusses other earlier literary versions of Saint Joan by Voltaire, Friedrich Schiller, Mark Twain, Andrew Lang and Anatole France. He identifies there what he sees as the shortcomings and inaccuracies of those versions.

Another precursor, which he may have known, was Tom Taylor's *Jeanne Darc (Called the Maid); a Chronicle Play, in Five Acts* (1871). He certainly knew *Jeanne d'Arc* (1906) by the American dramatist Percy Mackaye. George Bernard Shaw found this version untenably sentimental, despite the fact that it drew on the same historical source as his own play – T. Douglas Murray's translation of the transcription of trial documents made by Quicherat, entitled *Jeanne d'Arc, Maid of Orleans, Deliverer of France: Being the Story of Her Life, Her Achievements and Her Death, as Attested on Oath and Set Forth in the Original Documents* (1902).

NINETEENTH-CENTURY DRAMA

Popular theatrical taste in the nineteenth century gravitated towards **melodrama**, and to the 'well-made play'. The former specialised in sensational action and two-dimensional characterisation. Villainy and bloodlust were the staple of melodramas such as *Maria Marten; or The Murder in the Red Barn* (c. 1830), and *Sweeney Todd, the Demon Barber of Fleet Street* (1842). Middle-class audiences preferred the 'well-made play', neatly constructed, and eminently proper in content. George Bernard Shaw eschewed melodramatic devices, and rejected 'well-made' formulas.

HENRIK IBSEN

The polite yet hollow conventionality of the 'well-made play' was confronted significantly by the Scandinavian playwrights August Strindberg (1849–1912) and Henrik Ibsen (1828–1906). They led the way in forging a mode of drama grounded firmly in important issues of modern life. Their bold engagement with highly controversial, even taboo topics, issued a challenge to the hypocrisy which, in their view, posed as conventional morality. George Bernard Shaw drew encouragement from their pioneering example.

Henrik Ibsen called into question the institutions of marriage and the family. He criticised conformity and shallow respectability, and challenged stereotypical representation of women. In 1891, George Bernard Shaw published *The Quintessence of Ibsenism*, the first full-length study of the playwright in English. His continued importance for George Bernard Shaw was confirmed with the latter's revision of his pioneering study, in 1912–13.

PART SIX

CRITICAL HISTORY & BROADER PERSPECTIVES

CRITICAL HISTORY

George Bernard Shaw was sixty-seven years old when he completed *Saint Joan*. It was the last of his major plays, and many critics consider it his best. An account of the composition of the play is Brian Tyson's *The Story of Shaw's 'Saint Joan'* (McGill-Queen's UP, Kingston, 1982). The first performances of the play, in New York and in London, were notable popular successes. The New York production ran for 213 performances; the London run was 244. The New York première occurred late in December 1923. Critics in that city had been highly critical of George Bernard Shaw's previous play, *Back to Methuselah*, largely on account of its considerable length. *Saint Joan*, running at well over three hours, provoked similar objections. Generally the American reviews were mixed, with some critics intolerant of George Bernard Shaw's wordiness and concern for ideas rather than on-stage action. Others praised it highly. For example, Alexander Woollcott, in the *New York Herald*, found it engrossing, and saw greatness in the play.

The Italian playwright Luigi Pirandello was in the audience for that opening night, and supplied a commentary for the *New York Times*, in which he remarked upon the poetic quality of *Saint Joan*. He suggested that here, more than in any other play, George Bernard Shaw had allowed his artistry to override his need to convey a message or to indulge his humour. The commentary is reprinted in Stanley Weintraub's collection, *Saint Joan: Fifty Years After* (Louisiana State University Press, Baton Rouge, 1973).

That volume also contains contemporary assessments by Desmond MacCarthy and Edmund Wilson, amongst others. MacCarthy remarked upon the play's felicitous combination of seriousness and entertainment, and suggested that it might be George Bernard Shaw's greatest play. He described *Saint Joan* as not primarily a historical drama, but rather a religious play. Edmund Wilson noted with approval the even-handedness with which George Bernard Shaw had portrayed the representatives of authority and tradition, allowing them similar credibility to that granted to the unorthodox rebel.

Some early reviewers were uneasy about certain aspects of the play's language: the use of dialect and slang, and Joan's persistent recourse to nicknames. Prior to its opening performance in London, several critics, including A.B. Walkley in the *Times*, expressed hopes that the play would not be marred by those flippancies and **anachronisms** that were felt to have detracted from the value of his earlier forays into historical drama. The recent sanctification of Joan by the Vatican was perceived as a deeply serious event, not to be travestied by George Bernard Shaw's irreverent humour. After seeing it, Walkley praised the play, although registering dissatisfaction with the Epilogue. James Agate in the *Sunday Times* was less effusive, admiring the trial and the scene in the cathedral, but agreeing with Walkley that the Epilogue was unnecessary.

A number of early critics suggested that the Epilogue was in many ways redundant, as it seemed to repeat issues already addressed in the body of the play. It was widely felt to compromise the play's integrity. George Bernard Shaw responded directly to these criticisms in the Preface he wrote for the play in May 1924.

The French première of the play was preceded by debate as to whether George Bernard Shaw's version insulted the national heroine. It opened in Paris in April 1925. Ludmilla Pitoeff played the leading role, altering radically the emphases that George Bernard Shaw had placed on Joan's main characteristics. In place of his robust and energetic young woman, this Joan was delicate to the point of frailty. It ran nonetheless for over 100 performances, and has been produced regularly since then.

The Scottish writer and politician, J.M. Robertson published a book-length study of the play in 1925, *Mr Shaw and 'The Maid'*. He acknowledged that the play worked very well as a play, but he was highly critical of the manner in which George Bernard Shaw handled the reality of the historical incidents portrayed. In 1926, T.S. Eliot, emerging not only as a significant poet, but also as an extremely influential arbiter of literary taste, published an essay in the *Criterion*, in which he espoused the attack made by J.M. Robertson. T.S. Eliot argued that George Bernard Shaw had reduced the saint to the level of middle-class reformer. His essay, reproduced in Weintraub's collection, delivered a damaging blow to George Bernard Shaw's reputation amongst serious readers and theatregoers.

This situation was compounded by the adverse criticism levelled by the British Marxist, Raymond Williams, who argued that George Bernard Shaw had conveniently suppressed any sense of Joan's sexuality. He saw the play as damaged, despite its author's best intentions, by lapses into **melodrama** and sentimentality. During the 1970s and 1980s there was a concerted theatrical revival of George Bernard Shaw's plays in British theatres, but his eminence at the turn of the century has never been fully recovered. Nonetheless, *Saint Joan* is established as a major contribution to twentieth-century drama.

The reviews by A.B. Walkley and James Agate, a brief excerpt from J.M. Robertson's book, and Raymond Williams's essay can be found in the 'Casebook', *Bernard Shaw: Man and Superman and Saint Joan*, edited by A.M. Gibbs (1992). The volume also contains an essay by Daniel C. Gerould discussing the initial reception of the play when first performed in France in 1925.

Another helpful collation is *Shaw: The Critical Heritage*, edited by T.F. Evans (Routledge & Kegan Paul, 1976).

CONTEMPORARY APPROACHES

GENRE CRITICISM

A substantial number of essays have been devoted to the question of genre in relation to *Saint Joan*. Genre is a means of categorising literary works, differentiating between the characteristics of different kinds of writing, and defining their relationships within literary history. Clearly the major generic category to which *Saint Joan* belongs is drama. George Bernard Shaw's work was contemporaneous with innovative work in poetry and in the novel. T.S. Eliot's poem *The Waste Land* and James Joyce's novel *Ulysses* both appeared in 1922. Yet George Bernard Shaw seems to have been more keenly aware of Shakespeare, a fellow dramatist, than of those adventurous contemporaries, and critics have tended to focus upon the play's place in dramatic tradition, rather than its relationship to the experimental literary climate of the 1920s.

Debate has turned especially around whether *Saint Joan* belongs to the genre of tragedy or that of comedy, both subdivisions of the larger dramatic genre. Tragedy characteristically follows the rise and fall of a singular individual. The inevitability of the fall indicates human aspiration meeting its limits. Comedy invariably entails a happy ending, in which conflict is resolved, and members of a group are reconciled to harmonious coexistence.

Louis L. Martz approached the issue through comparison with one of T.S. Eliot's plays in his essay, 'The Saint as Tragic Hero: *Saint Joan* and *Murder in the Cathedral*'. He asks whether it can be appropriate to regard a saint as a tragic figure, given that sainthood is a fate that can scarcely be lamented. His discussion of the problem can be found in *George Bernard Shaw's 'Saint Joan'* (Chelsea House, 1987), edited by Harold Bloom for the 'Modern Critical Interpretations' series.

The volume contains another reading of the play's generic status: Charles A. Berst's '*Saint Joan*: Spiritual Epic as Tragicomedy'. Berst locates George Bernard Shaw's work firmly in the hybrid genre of the tragicomic, a blending of tragic and comic elements. Harold Bloom also includes Margery A. Moran's essay 'The Histories', which considers *Saint Joan* as an example of the genre of historical drama. She identifies the characteristics that the play shares with George Bernard Shaw's other history plays.

FEMINIST CRITICISM

An important aspect of feminist literary criticism has been analysis of ways in which male authors have represented women. This approach has been particularly concerned with criticising the use of stereotypes or other forms of reductive characterisation to support the relegation of women to marginal or subordinate roles within a society dominated by men. In the Preface, George Bernard Shaw observes that:

> If a historian is an Anti-Feminist, and does not believe women to be capable of
> genius in the traditional masculine departments, he will never make anything of

> Joan, whose genius was turned to practical account mainly in soldiering and
> politics. (p. 10)

Feminist criticism of George Bernard Shaw initially voiced approval of
his rejection of repressive Victorian ideals, and spoke favourably of his
realistic depiction of situations faced by contemporary women.

As well as evaluating the degree to which George Bernard Shaw's
approach to characterisation of Joan has succeeded in meeting such goals,
feminist reading can find a great deal to analyse within the play. For
example, the threat by Joan's father to drown his daughter if she persisted
in aspiring to become a soldier can be seen as a crude assertion of
patriarchal authority; that is, of male social dominance, following the
model of the father as unquestioned head of a family. The fact that Joan
later struggles to win acceptance among those men who act as figures of
authority manifests a deeply engrained resistance to women, especially
young ones, assuming positions of power and influence. Although Joan
readily argues that she is adept in 'the household arts of the mistresses of
well furnished houses' (p. 77), she makes it clear that she is far from
content to remain at home, spinning and weaving in the manner expected
of women.

Joan insists on dressing like a soldier, and her clothing is indicative
of her refusal to be excluded from conventionally male roles. This act of
defiance is regularly criticised by male figures of authority in the play. It
is notable that the trial is conducted exclusively by men, and of course the
priesthood was a male domain. Feminist criticism draws attention to this
conventional distribution of social power, and highlights its
oppressiveness to women.

Barbara Bellow Watson in *A Shavian Guide to the Intelligent Woman*
(Norton, 1972; first published 1964) was the first to place exclusive
emphasis upon women in George Bernard Shaw's work. Sonia Lorichs
developed the analysis in *The Unwomanly Woman in Bernard Shaw's
Drama and Her Social and Political Background* (Uppsala University
Press, 1973). Rodelle Weintraub edited a collection of essays entitled
Fabian Feminist: Bernard Shaw and Woman (Pennsylvania State
University Press, 1977). Margot Peters wrote a supportive critical
biography, *Bernard Shaw and the Actresses* (Doubleday, 1980). Of late,

feminist analysis has been less unequivocally supportive of George Bernard Shaw's service to the cause of women. J. Ellen Gainor, in *Shaw's Daughters* (University of Michigan Press, Ann Arbor, 1991), finds the playwright a less progressive figure, firmly rooted in Victorian thinking.

Carolyn Heilbrun, in *Toward A Recognition Of Androgyny* (Knopf, 1973), noted that George Bernard Shaw had created his Joan as an androgynous figure, combining characteristics customarily associated with both femininity and masculinity. He was thus challenging conventional exclusion of women from activities invariably assigned to men. In addition, he was challenging the notion that men should not share conventionally feminine characteristics, such as sensitivity and compassion.

More recent feminist criticism has sought to break the conventional associations of masculinity and femininity with particular characteristics or abilities. So instead of saying that Joan combines the qualities of man and woman, such criticism calls into question the notion of clear-cut division of attributes along gender lines.

MARXIST CRITICISM

As a Fabian socialist, George Bernard Shaw was far more at home amongst middle-class intellectuals than working-class revolutionaries, and although he sympathised in broad terms with the goals of Karl Marx's Communist philosophy, he differed with it in very significant respects. George Bernard Shaw saw the middle class as the breeding ground for social change, and increasingly he placed emphasis upon the individual as a catalyst for historical development. This is reflected in *Saint Joan*. It is stressed that Joan comes from the middle ranks of society, and it is her individualistic outlook that makes her an agent of the Life Force.

Marxist analysis would be critical of this shift of emphasis in George Bernard Shaw's work away from the agency of the working class as a whole. The first three scenes may be said to trace a popular uprising against the oppressive powers of the Church and the ruling class. Emphasis is largely upon action, and this would suit Marxist emphasis upon material events, directed towards liberation. The apparent mysticism of Joan, however, and George Bernard Shaw's insistence upon her as the principal focus of the drama would be considered a betrayal of the solidarity of working-class identity. Instead of heroic class struggle, *Saint Joan* traces the development of a cult of personality around a charismatic heroine. Her eventual isolation follows inevitably from this flawed emphasis, which removes her from the cause of the people she initially represents.

The enemies of the working class in Marx's view, the priests and the nobility, are portrayed by George Bernard Shaw as fair-minded and balanced in their trial of the insurgent woman. The Marxist critic would consider this as a fatal accommodation of the oppressors by an essentially bourgeois writer. This has been compounded by the coronation of a king whose only interest is self-preservation. The concluding Epilogue veers from decadent idolatry, the ultimate manifestation of the personality cult, to the predictable return of Joan's isolation. At the end she appears as an idealistic visionary rather than a palpable motive force to effect real social change. The departure from a realistic mode of representation in the Epilogue would be seen by a Marxist as symptomatic of George Bernard Shaw's failure to be true to material historical processes.

A Marxist reading would thus find much to criticise in George Bernard Shaw's historical drama. But it would approve of his recognition that conflict is the motor of history, and of his concentration upon the need to work towards a just future society, rather than offering support to the *status quo*. A more extended reading of this kind may be found in Alick West's essay, '*Saint Joan*: A Marxist View', collected in Stanley Weintraub's book *Saint Joan: Fifty Years After* (Louisiana State University Press, 1973).

World events		Author's life	Literary context
End of First World War Civil war in Russia	1918		*Eminent Victorians* by Lytton Strachey
Hitler founds National Socialist German Workers' Party in Germany Benito Mussolini founds Fascist Party in Italy Lady Astor becomes first female MP	1919	*Heartbreak House* is performed and published	*Night and Day* by Virginia Woolf *Caesar's Wife* by W. Somerset Maugham
Joan of Arc canonised by Pope Benedict XV Government of Ireland Act divides Ireland into two self-governing areas	1920	*Irish Nationalism and Labour Internationalism* is published	*Women in Love* by D.H. Lawrence *Beyond the Horizon* by Eugene O'Neill *The Age of Innocence* by Edith Wharton
Irish Free State established	1921	*Back to Methuselah* is published	*Six Characters in Search of An Author* by Luigi Pirandello *Four Plays for Dancers* by W.B. Yeats
	1922		*Ulysses* by James Joyce published in Paris (UK publication, 1936) *Hassan* by James Elroy Flecker *The Waste Land* by T.S.Eliot

World events		Author's life	Literary context
Benito Mussolini creates Fascist state in Italy	**1923**	*Saint Joan* is first produced in New York	*The Shadow of a Gunman* by Sean O'Casey
Lenin dies	**1924**	*Saint Joan* is produced in London and published with Preface	*The Vortex* by Noel Coward
			Juno and the Paycock by Sean O'Casey
			Desire Under the Elms by Eugene O'Neill
	1925	George Bernard Shaw wins the Nobel Prize for Literature	*The Great Gatsby* by F. Scott Fitzgerald
		J.M. Robertson publishes *Mr Shaw and 'The Maid'*, a book-length study of *Saint Joan*	*Hay Fever* by Noel Coward
			The Trial by Franz Kafka
General Strike in Britain	**1926**	T.S. Eliot essay about George Bernard Shaw is published in the *Criterion*	*The Plough and the Stars* by Sean O'Casey
	1927		*To the Lighthouse* by Virginia Woolf
Equal Franchise Act gives women over twenty-one the vote in Britain	**1928**	*The Intelligent Woman's Guide to Socialism* is published	*Lady Chatterley's Lover* by D.H. Lawrence is printed privately in Italy
			Decline and Fall by Evelyn Waugh
			Journey's End by R.C. Sherrif

anachronism the introduction into the account of one historical period of elements drawn from another or others

chronicle play a play that follows the unfolding of an actual sequence of historical events

irony saying one thing while meaning another; or, the presentation of one interpretation of events on stage, while allowing the audience to make another, different interpretation

melodrama plays that present sensational events, improbable happenings, and violent action, more or less to the exclusion of other materials

romance tales of chivalry and love, untarnished by reference to harsher realities

satire a work, often savagely funny, designed to expose the follies and foibles of human beings, especially those in positions of power and members of polite or fashionable society

soliloquy a speech delivered by a character alone on stage

symbol one thing standing for another, by analogy or association; so, a rose has traditionally been symbolic of beauty

Author of this note

Dr Julian Cowley taught at King's College London before joining the University of Luton, where he is Senior Lecturer in Literary Studies.

NOTES

NOTES

NOTES

York Notes Advanced (£3.99 each)

Margaret Atwood
The Handmaid's Tale

Jane Austen
Mansfield Park

Jane Austen
Persuasion

Jane Austen
Pride and Prejudice

Alan Bennett
Talking Heads

William Blake
Songs of Innocence and of Experience

Charlotte Brontë
Jane Eyre

Emily Brontë
Wuthering Heights

Geoffrey Chaucer
The Franklin's Tale

Geoffrey Chaucer
General Prologue to the Canterbury Tales

Geoffrey Chaucer
The Wife of Bath's Prologue and Tale

Joseph Conrad
Heart of Darkness

Charles Dickens
Great Expectations

John Donne
Selected Poems

George Eliot
The Mill on the Floss

F. Scott Fitzgerald
The Great Gatsby

E.M. Forster
A Passage to India

Brian Friel
Translations

Thomas Hardy
The Mayor of Casterbridge

Thomas Hardy
Tess of the d'Urbervilles

Seamus Heaney
Selected Poems from Opened Ground

Nathaniel Hawthorne
The Scarlet Letter

James Joyce
Dubliners

John Keats
Selected Poems

Christopher Marlowe
Doctor Faustus

Arthur Miller
Death of a Salesman

Toni Morrison
Beloved

William Shakespeare
Antony and Cleopatra

William Shakespeare
As You Like It

William Shakespeare
Hamlet

William Shakespeare
King Lear

William Shakespeare
Measure for Measure

William Shakespeare
The Merchant of Venice

William Shakespeare
Much Ado About Nothing

William Shakespeare
Othello

William Shakespeare
Romeo and Juliet

William Shakespeare
The Tempest

William Shakespeare
The Winter's Tale

Mary Shelley
Frankenstein

Alice Walker
The Color Purple

Oscar Wilde
The Importance of Being Earnest

Tennessee Williams
A Streetcar Named Desire

John Webster
The Duchess of Malfi

W.B. Yeats
Selected Poems

GCSE and equivalent levels (£3.50 each)

Maya Angelou
I Know Why the Caged Bird Sings

Jane Austen
Pride and Prejudice

Alan Ayckbourn
Absent Friends

Elizabeth Barrett Browning
Selected Poems

Robert Bolt
A Man for All Seasons

Harold Brighouse
Hobson's Choice

Charlotte Brontë
Jane Eyre

Emily Brontë
Wuthering Heights

Shelagh Delaney
A Taste of Honey

Charles Dickens
David Copperfield

Charles Dickens
Great Expectations

Charles Dickens
Hard Times

Charles Dickens
Oliver Twist

Roddy Doyle
Paddy Clarke Ha Ha Ha

George Eliot
Silas Marner

George Eliot
The Mill on the Floss

William Golding
Lord of the Flies

Oliver Goldsmith
She Stoops To Conquer

Willis Hall
The Long and the Short and the Tall

Thomas Hardy
Far from the Madding Crowd

Thomas Hardy
The Mayor of Casterbridge

Thomas Hardy
Tess of the d'Urbervilles

Thomas Hardy
The Withered Arm and other Wessex Tales

L.P. Hartley
The Go-Between

Seamus Heaney
Selected Poems

Susan Hill
I'm the King of the Castle

Barry Hines
A Kestrel for a Knave

Louise Lawrence
Children of the Dust

Harper Lee
To Kill a Mockingbird

Laurie Lee
Cider with Rosie

Arthur Miller
The Crucible

Arthur Miller
A View from the Bridge

Robert O'Brien
Z for Zachariah

Frank O'Connor
My Oedipus Complex and other stories

George Orwell
Animal Farm

J.B. Priestley
An Inspector Calls

Willy Russell
Educating Rita

Willy Russell
Our Day Out

J.D. Salinger
The Catcher in the Rye

William Shakespeare
Henry IV Part 1

William Shakespeare
Henry V

William Shakespeare
Julius Caesar

William Shakespeare
Macbeth

William Shakespeare
The Merchant of Venice

William Shakespeare
A Midsummer Night's Dream

William Shakespeare
Much Ado About Nothing

William Shakespeare
Romeo and Juliet

William Shakespeare
The Tempest

William Shakespeare
Twelfth Night

George Bernard Shaw
Pygmalion

Mary Shelley
Frankenstein

R.C. Sherriff
Journey's End

Rukshana Smith
Salt on the snow

John Steinbeck
Of Mice and Men

Robert Louis Stevenson
Dr Jekyll and Mr Hyde

Jonathan Swift
Gulliver's Travels

Robert Swindells
Daz 4 Zoe

Mildred D. Taylor
Roll of Thunder, Hear My Cry

Mark Twain
Huckleberry Finn

James Watson
Talking in Whispers

William Wordsworth
Selected Poems

A Choice of Poets

Mystery Stories of the Nineteenth Century including The Signalman

Nineteenth Century Short Stories

Poetry of the First World War

Six Women Poets

Chinua Achebe
Things Fall Apart

Edward Albee
Who's Afraid of Virginia Woolf?

Margaret Atwood
Cat's Eye

Jane Austen
Emma

Jane Austen
Northanger Abbey

Jane Austen
Sense and Sensibility

Samuel Beckett
Waiting for Godot

Robert Browning
Selected Poems

Robert Burns
Selected Poems

Angela Carter
Nights at the Circus

Geoffrey Chaucer
The Merchant's Tale

Geoffrey Chaucer
The Miller's Tale

Geoffrey Chaucer
The Nun's Priest's Tale

Samuel Taylor Coleridge
Selected Poems

Daniel Defoe
Moll Flanders

Daniel Defoe
Robinson Crusoe

Charles Dickens
Bleak House

Charles Dickens
Hard Times

Emily Dickinson
Selected Poems

Carol Ann Duffy
Selected Poems

George Eliot
Middlemarch

T.S. Eliot
The Waste Land

T.S. Eliot
Selected Poems

Henry Fielding
Joseph Andrews

E.M. Forster
Howards End

John Fowles
The French Lieutenant's Woman

Robert Frost
Selected Poems

Elizabeth Gaskell
North and South

Stella Gibbons
Cold Comfort Farm

Graham Greene
Brighton Rock

Thomas Hardy
Jude the Obscure

Thomas Hardy
Selected Poems

Joseph Heller
Catch-22

Homer
The Iliad

Homer
The Odyssey

Gerard Manley Hopkins
Selected Poems

Aldous Huxley
Brave New World

Kazuo Ishiguro
The Remains of the Day

Ben Jonson
The Alchemist

Ben Jonson
Volpone

James Joyce
A Portrait of the Artist as a Young Man

Philip Larkin
Selected Poems

D.H. Lawrence
The Rainbow

D.H. Lawrence
Selected Stories

D.H. Lawrence
Sons and Lovers

D.H. Lawrence
Women in Love

John Milton
Paradise Lost Bks I & II

John Milton
Paradise Lost Bks IV & IX

Thomas More
Utopia

Sean O'Casey
Juno and the Paycock

George Orwell
Nineteen Eighty-four

John Osborne
Look Back in Anger

Wilfred Owen
Selected Poems

Sylvia Plath
Selected Poems

Alexander Pope
Rape of the Lock and other poems

Ruth Prawer Jhabvala
Heat and Dust

Jean Rhys
Wide Sargasso Sea

William Shakespeare
As You Like It

William Shakespeare
Coriolanus

William Shakespeare
Henry IV Pt 1

William Shakespeare
Henry V

William Shakespeare
Julius Caesar

William Shakespeare
Macbeth

William Shakespeare
Measure for Measure

William Shakespeare
A Midsummer Night's Dream

William Shakespeare
Richard II

William Shakespeare
Richard III

William Shakespeare
Sonnets

William Shakespeare
The Taming of the Shrew

William Shakespeare
Twelfth Night

William Shakespeare
The Winter's Tale

George Bernard Shaw
Arms and the Man

George Bernard Shaw
Saint Joan

Muriel Spark
The Prime of Miss Jean Brodie

John Steinbeck
The Grapes of Wrath

John Steinbeck
The Pearl

Tom Stoppard
Arcadia

Tom Stoppard
*Rosencrantz and Guildenstern
are Dead*

Jonathan Swift
*Gulliver's Travels and The
Modest Proposal*

Alfred, Lord Tennyson
Selected Poems

W.M. Thackeray
Vanity Fair

Virgil
The Aeneid

Edith Wharton
The Age of Innocence

Tennessee Williams
Cat on a Hot Tin Roof

Tennessee Williams
The Glass Menagerie

Virginia Woolf
Mrs Dalloway

Virginia Woolf
To the Lighthouse

William Wordsworth
Selected Poems

Metaphysical Poets

York Notes – the Ultimate Literature Guides

York Notes are recognised as the best literature study guides.
If you have enjoyed using this book and have found it useful, you
can now order others directly from us – simply follow the ordering
instructions below.

HOW TO ORDER

Decide which title(s) you require and then order in one of the following
ways:

Booksellers
All titles available from good bookstores.

By post
List the title(s) you require in the space provided overleaf,
select your method of payment, complete your name and
address details and return your completed order form and
payment to:

> *Addison Wesley Longman Ltd*
> *PO BOX 88*
> *Harlow*
> *Essex CM19 5SR*

By phone
Call our Customer Information Centre on 01279 623923 to
place your order, quoting mail number: HEYN1.

By fax
Complete the order form overleaf, ensuring you fill in your
name and address details and method of payment, and fax it
to us on 01279 414130.

By e-mail
E-mail your order to us on awlhe.orders@awl.co.uk listing
title(s) and quantity required and providing full name and
address details as requested overleaf. Please quote mail
number: HEYN1. Please do not send credit card details by
e-mail.

York Notes Order Form

Titles required:

Quantity	Title/ISBN	Price

Sub total _____

Please add £2.50 postage & packing _____

(P & P is free for orders over £50) _____

Total _____

Mail no: HEYN1

Your Name _____

Your Address _____

_____

Postcode _____ Telephone _____

Method of payment

☐ I enclose a cheque or a P/O for £_____ made payable to
Addison Wesley Longman Ltd

☐ Please charge my Visa/Access/AMEX/Diners Club card
Number _____ Expiry Date _____
Signature _____ Date _____

(please ensure that the address given above is the same as for your credit card)

Prices and other details are correct at time of going to press but may change without notice. All orders are subject to status.

☐ *Please tick this box if you would like a complete listing of Longman Study Guides (suitable for GCSE and A-level students)*

🌐 York Press

📘 Longman

Addison
Wesley
Longman